# Video Game Development: A Career Guide

# Video Game Development: A Career Guide

### Arnold Rhinegold

Larsen & Keller
www.larsen-keller.com

Video Game Development: A Career Guide
Arnold Rhinegold
ISBN: 979-8-88836-097-2 (Hardback)

Larsen & Keller
Published by Larsen and Keller Education,
5 Penn Plaza,
19th Floor,
New York, NY 10001, USA

**Cataloging-in-Publication Data**

Video game development : a career guide / Arnold Rhinegold.
    p. cm.
Includes bibliographical references and index.
ISBN 979-8-88836-097-2
1. Video games--Design--Vocational guidance. 2. Video game designers--Vocational guidance.
I. Rhinegold, Arnold
GV1469.3 .V53 2023
794.8--dc23

For more information regarding Larsen and Keller Education and its products, please visit the publisher's website www.larsen-keller.com

# Table of Contents

**Permissions**

**Index**

# Preface

Video game development is the process by which a video game is created. It can be a console game or a commercial PC game, or an Indie game. The gaming industry has seen significant growth owing to the rise of new online distribution systems and the mobile game market, for iOS and Android devices. Console games and mainstream PC games all follow a sequence of developmental phases. These include pre-production, production, milestones and post-production stages. Various roles are intrinsic to video game development, such as designers, programmers, artists, level designers, testers and sound engineers. This textbook elucidates the innovative models around prospective developments with respect to video game development. Selected concepts that redefine this field have been presented herein. As this field is emerging at a rapid pace, the contents of this book will help the readers understand the diverse career opportunities in this dynamic field, and how to pursue them.

Given below is the chapter wise description of the book:

Chapter 1- A video game developer is a professional who specializes in video game development. It encompasses individual aspects of programming, design, testing, etc. A developer may specialize in particular consoles such as Microsoft's Xbox One, Nintendo's Nintendo Switch, Sony's PlayStation 4, etc. This chapter introduces in brief about the career pathway of a video game developer, and the ways to become a video game programmer or an artist for video games.

Chapter 2- Video game development is a software development process Game development involves an integration of agile development and Personal Software Process (PSP). Several pre-production, production and post-production processes are involved. The topics elaborated in this chapter cover the various processes of video game development such as programming a video game, designing a successful platforming game, making a simple PC video game, coding video game, making a video game side quest, etc.

Chapter 3- Video games can be classified into three important categories- casual games, serious games and educational games. This chapter examines the different types of video games such as flash games, educational games, virtual games, CMD adventure, etc. and the ways to create them.

Chapter 4- The choice of design and development tools can help to create an exciting video game. Due to the development atmosphere of virtual reality application and fast-paced gaming environment, there has been tremendous innovation in gaming software and tools. The content in this chapter on making video games with Klik and Play, CMD and Unity 5 will facilitate the understanding of some of the tools and software used for video game development.

Indeed, my job was extremely crucial and challenging as I had to ensure that every chapter is informative and structured in a student-friendly manner. I am thankful for the support provided by my family and colleagues during the completion of this book.

**Arnold Rhinegold**

# Becoming a Video Game Developer

A video game developer is a professional who specializes in video game development. It encompasses individual aspects of programming, design, testing, etc. A developer may specialize in particular consoles such as Microsoft's Xbox One, Nintendo's Nintendo Switch, Sony's PlayStation 4, etc. This chapter introduces in brief about the career pathway of a video game developer, and the ways to become a video game programmer or an artist for video games.

## Video Game Development

Video game development is the process of creating a video game. The effort is undertaken by a game developer, who may range from a single person to an international team dispersed across the globe. Traditional commercial PC and console games are normally funded by a publisher, and can take several years to reach completion. Indie games can take less time and can be produced at a lower cost by individuals and smaller developers. The independent game industry has seen a substantial rise in recent years with the growth of new online distribution systems, such as Steam and Uplay, as well as the mobile game market, such as for Android and iOS devices.

The first video games were non-commercial, and were developed in the 1960s. They required mainframe computers to run and were not available to the general public. Commercial game development began in the 1970s with the advent of first-generation video game consoles and early home computers like the Apple I. Due to low costs and low capabilities of computers, a lone programmer could develop a full game. However, approaching the 21st century, ever-increasing computer processing power and heightened consumer expectations made it difficult for a single person to produce a mainstream console or PC game. The average cost of producing a triple-A video game slowly rose from US$1–4 million in 2000 to over $5 million in 2006, then to over $20 million by 2010.

Mainstream PC and console games are generally developed in phases. First, in pre-production, pitches, prototypes, and game design documents are written. If the idea is approved and the developer receives funding, a full-scale development begins. This usually involves a team of 20–100 individuals with various responsibilities, including designers, artists, programmers, and testers.

Games are produced through the software development process. Games are developed as a creative outlet and to generate profit. Development is normally funded by a publisher. Well-made games bring profit more readily. However, it is important to estimate a game's financial requirements, such as development costs of individual features. Failing to provide clear implications of game's expectations may result in exceeding allocated budget. In fact, the majority of commercial games do not produce profit. Most developers cannot afford changing development schedule and require estimating their capabilities with available resources before production.

The game industry requires innovations, as publishers cannot profit from constant release of repetitive sequels and imitations. Every year new independent development companies open and some manage to develop hit titles. Similarly, many developers close down because they cannot find a publishing contract or their production is not profitable. It is difficult to start a new company due to high initial investment required. Nevertheless, growth of casual and mobile game market has allowed developers with smaller teams to enter the market. Once the companies become financially stable, they may expand to develop larger games. Most developers start small and gradually expand their business. A developer receiving profit from a successful title may store up a capital to expand and re-factor their company, as well as tolerate more failed deadlines.

An average development budget for a multiplatform game is US$18-28M, with high-profile games often exceeding $40M.

In the early era of home computers and video game consoles in the early 1980s, a single programmer could handle almost all the tasks of developing a game — programming, graphical design, sound effects, etc. It could take as little as six weeks to develop a game. However, the high user expectations and requirements of modern commercial games far exceed the capabilities of a single developer and require the splitting of responsibilities. A team of over a hundred people can be employed full-time for a single project.

Game development, production, or design is a process that starts from an idea or concept. Often the idea is based on a modification of an existing game concept. The game idea may fall within one or several genres. Designers often experiment with different combinations of genres. A game designer generally writes an initial game proposal document, that describes the basic concept, gameplay, feature list, setting and story, target audience, requirements and schedule, and finally staff and budget estimates. Different companies have different formal procedures and philosophies regarding game design and development. There is no standardized development method; however commonalities exist.

A game developer may range from a single individual to a large multinational company. There are both independent and publisher-owned studios. Independent developers rely on financial support from a game publisher. They usually have to develop a game from concept to prototype without external funding. The formal game proposal is then submitted to publishers, who may finance the game development from several months to years. The publisher would retain exclusive rights to distribute and market the game and would often own the intellectual property rights for the game franchise. Publisher's company may also own the developer's company, or it may have internal development studio(s). Generally the publisher is the one who owns the game's intellectual property rights.

All but the smallest developer companies work on several titles at once. This is necessary because of the time taken between shipping a game and receiving royalty payments, which may be between 6 and 18 months. Small companies may structure contracts, ask for advances on royalties, use shareware distribution, employ part-time workers and use other methods to meet payroll demands.

Console manufacturers, such as Microsoft, Nintendo, or Sony, have a standard set of technical requirements that a game must conform to in order to be approved. Additionally, the game concept must be approved by the manufacturer, who may refuse to approve certain titles.

Most modern PC or console games take from one to three years to complete., where as a mobile game can be developed in a few months. The length of development is influenced by a number of factors, such as genre, scale, development platform and number of assets.

Some games can take much longer than the average time frame to complete. An infamous example is 3D Realms' *Duke Nukem Forever*, announced to be in production in April 1997 and released fourteen years later in June 2011. Planning for Maxis' game *Spore* began in late 1999; the game was released nine years later in September 2008. The game *Prey* was briefly profiled in a 1997 issue of PC Gamer, but was not released until 2006, and only then in highly altered form. Finally, *Team Fortress 2* was in development from 1998 until its 2007 release, and emerged from a convoluted development process involving "probably three or four different games", according to Gabe Newell.

The game revenue from retails is divided among the parties along the distribution chain, such as — developer, publisher, retail, manufacturer and console royalty. Many developers fail to profit from this and go bankrupt. Many developers seek alternative economic models through Internet marketing and distribution channels to improve returns., as through a mobile distribution channel the share of a developer can be up to 70% of the total revenue  and through an online distribution channel almost 100%.

## Roles

### Producer

Development is overseen by internal and external producers. The producer working for the developer is known as the *internal producer* and manages the development team, schedules, reports progress, hires and assigns staff, and so on. The producer working for the publisher is known as the *external producer* and oversees developer progress and budget. Producer's responsibilities include PR, contract negotiation, liaising between the staff and stakeholders, schedule and budget maintenance, quality assurance, beta test management, and localization. This role may also be referred to as *project manager*, *project lead*, or *director*.

### Publisher

A video game publisher is a company that publishes video games that they have either developed internally or have had developed by an external video game developer. As with book publishers or publishers of DVD movies, video game publishers are responsible for their product's manufacturing and marketing, including market research and all aspects of advertising.

They usually finance the development, sometimes by paying a video game developer (the publisher calls this external development) and sometimes by paying an internal staff of developers called a studio. Consequently, they also typically own the IP of the game. Large video game publishers also distribute the games they publish, while some smaller publishers instead hire distribution companies (or larger video game publishers) to distribute the games they publish.

Other functions usually performed by the publisher include deciding on and paying for any license that the game may utilize; paying for localization; layout, printing, and possibly the writing of the user manual; and the creation of graphic design elements such as the box design.

Large publishers may also attempt to boost efficiency across all internal and external development teams by providing services such as sound design and code packages for commonly needed functionality.

Because the publisher usually finances development, it usually tries to manage development risk with a staff of producers or project managers to monitor the progress of the developer, critique ongoing development, and assist as necessary. Most video games created by an external video game developer are paid for with periodic advances on royalties. These advances are paid when the developer reaches certain stages of development, called milestones.

Independent video game developers create games without a publisher and may choose to digitally distribute their games.

## Development Team

Developers can range in size from small groups making casual games to housing hundreds of employees and producing several large titles. Companies divide their subtasks of game's development. Individual job titles may vary; however, roles are the same within the industry. The development team consists of several members. Some members of the team may handle more than one role; similarly more than one task may be handled by the same member. Team size can vary from 20 to 100 or more members, depending on the game's scope. The most represented are artists, followed by programmers, then designers, and finally, audio specialists, with two to three producers in management. These positions are employed full-time. Other positions, such as testers, may be employed only part-time. Salaries for these positions vary depending on both the experience and the location of the employee. An entry-level programmer can make, on average, around $70,000 annually and an experienced programmer can make, on average, around $125,000 annually.

A development team includes these roles or disciplines:

## Designer

A game designer is a person who designs gameplay, conceiving and designing the rules and structure of a game. Development teams usually have a lead designer who coordinates the work of other designers. They are the main visionary of the game. One of the roles of a designer is being a writer, often employed part-time to conceive game's narrative, dialogue, commentary, cutscene narrative, journals, video game packaging content, hint system, etc. In larger projects, there are often separate designers for various parts of the game, such as, game mechanics, user interface, characters, dialogue, etc.

## Artist

A game artist is a visual artist who creates video game art. The art production is usually overseen by an *art director* or *art lead*, making sure their vision is followed. The art director manages the art team, scheduling and coordinating within the development team.

The artist's job may be 2D oriented or 3D oriented. *2D artists* may produce concept art, sprites, textures, environmental backdrops or terrain images, and user interface. *3D artists* may produce models or meshes, animation, 3D environment, and cinematics. Artists sometimes occupy both roles.

## Programmer

A game programmer is a software engineer who primarily develops video games or related software (such as game development tools). The game's codebase development is handled by programmers. There are usually one to several lead programmers, who implement the game's starting codebase and overview future development and programmer allocation on individual modules.

Individual programming disciplines roles include:

- Physics – the programming of the game engine, including simulating physics, collision, object movement, etc.
- AI – producing computer agents using game AI techniques, such as scripting, planning, rule-based decisions, etc.
- Graphics – the managing of graphical content utilization and memory considerations; the production of graphics engine, integration of models, textures to work along the physics engine.
- Sound – integration of music, speech, effect sounds into the proper locations and times.
- Gameplay – implementation of various games rules and features (sometimes called a *generalist*).
- Scripting – development and maintenance of high-level command system for various in-game tasks, such as AI, level editor triggers, etc.
- UI – production of user interface elements, like option menus, HUDs, help and feedback systems, etc.
- Input processing – processing and compatibility correlation of various input devices, such as keyboard, mouse, gamepad, etc.
- Network communications – the managing of data inputs and outputs for local and internet gameplay.
- Game tools – the production of tools to accompany the development of the game, especially for designers and scripters.

## Level Designer

A level designer is a person who creates levels, challenges or missions for computer and/or video games using a specific set of programs. These programs may be commonly available commercial 3D or 2D design programs, or specially designed and tailored level editors made for a specific game.

Level designers work with both incomplete and complete versions of the game. Game programmers usually produce level editors and design tools for the designers to use. This eliminates the need for designers to access or modify game code. Level editors may involve custom high-level scripting languages for interactive environments or AIs. As opposed to the level editing tools sometimes available to the community, level designers often work with placeholders and prototypes aiming for consistency and clear layout before required artwork is completed.

## Sound engineer

Sound engineers are technical professionals responsible for sound effects and sound positioning. They sometimes oversee voice acting and other sound asset creation. Composers who create a game's musical score also comprise a game's sound team, though often this work is outsourced.

## Tester

The quality assurance is carried out by game testers. A game tester analyzes video games to document software defects as part of a quality control. Testing is a highly technical field requiring computing expertise, and analytic competence.

The testers ensure that the game falls within the proposed design: it both works and is entertaining.This involves testing of all features, compatibility, localization, etc. Although, necessary throughout the whole development process, testing is expensive and is often actively utilized only towards the completion of the project.

## Development Process

Game development is a software development process, as a video game is software with art, audio, and gameplay. Formal software development methods are often overlooked. Games with poor development methodology are likely to run over budget and time estimates, as well as contain a large number of bugs. Planning is important for individual and group projects alike.

Overall game development is not suited for typical software life cycle methods, such as the waterfall model.

One method employed for game development is agile development. It is based on iterative prototyping, a subset of software prototyping. Agile development depends on feedback and refinement of game's iterations with gradually increasing feature set. This method is effective because most projects do not start with a clear requirement outline. A popular method of agile software development is Scrum.

Another successful method is Personal Software Process (PSP) requiring additional training for staff to increase awareness of project's planning. This method is more expensive and requires commitment of team members. PSP can be extended to Team Software Process, where the whole team is self-directing.

Game development usually involves an overlap of these methods. For example, asset creation may be done via waterfall model, because requirements and specification are clear,  but gameplay design might be done using iterative prototyping.

Development of a commercial game usually includes the following stages:

## Pre-production

Pre-production or design phase is a planning phase of the project focused on idea and concept development and production of initial design documents. The goal of concept development is to produce clear and easy to understand documentation, which describes all the tasks, schedules and estimates for the development team. The suite of documents produced in this phase is called production plan. This phase is usually not funded by a publisher, however good publishers may require developers to produce plans during pre-production.

The concept documentation can be separated into three stages or documents—high concept, pitch and concept; however, there is no industry standard naming convention, for example, both Bethke (2003) and Bates (2004) refer to *pitch document* as "game proposal", yet Moore, Novak (2010) refers to *concept document* as "game proposal".

The late stage of pre-production may also be referred to as *proof of concept*, or *technical review* when more detailed game documents are produced.

Publishers have started to expect broader game proposals even featuring playable prototypes.

## High Concept

High concept is a brief description of a game. The high concept is the one-or two-sentence response to the question, "What is your game about?".

## Pitch

A pitch, concept document, proposal document, or game proposal is a short summary document intended to present the game's selling points and detail why the game would be profitable to develop.

Verbal pitches may be made to management within the developer company, and then presented to publishers. A written document may need to be shown to publishers before funding is approved. A game proposal may undergo one to several green-light meetings with publisher executives who determine if the game is to be developed. The presentation of the project is often given by the game designers. Demos may be created for the pitch; however may be unnecessary for established developers with good track records.

If the developer acts as its own publisher, or both companies are subsidiaries of a single company, then only the upper management needs to give approval.

## Concept

Concept document, game proposal, or game plan is a more detailed document than the pitch document. This includes all the information produced about the game. This includes the high concept, game's genre, gameplay description, features, setting, story, target audience, hardware platforms, estimated schedule, marketing analysis, team requirements, and risk analysis.

Before an approved design is completed, a skeleton crew of programmers and artists usually begins work. Programmers may develop quick-and-dirty prototypes showcasing one or more features that stakeholders would like to see incorporated in the final product. Artists may develop concept art and asset sketches as a springboard for developing real game assets. Producers may work part-time on the game at this point, scaling up for full-time commitment as development progresses. Game producers work during pre-production is related to planning the schedule, budget and estimating tasks with the team. The producer aims to create a solid production plan so that no delays are experienced at the start of the production.

## Game Design Document

Before a full-scale production can begin, the development team produces the first version of a game design document incorporating all or most of the material from the initial pitch. The design document describes the game's concept and major gameplay elements in detail. It may also include preliminary sketches of various aspects of the game. The design document is sometimes accompanied by functional prototypes of some sections of the game. The design document remains a living document throughout the development—often changed weekly or even daily.

Compiling a list of game's needs is called "requirement capture".

## Prototype

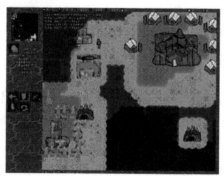

Placeholder graphics are characteristic of early game prototypes.

Writing prototypes of gameplay ideas and features is an important activity that allows programmers and game designers to experiment with different algorithms and usability scenarios for a game. A great deal of prototyping may take place during pre-production before the design document is complete and may, in fact, help determine what features the design specifies. Prototyping at this stage is often done manually, (paper prototyping), not digitally, as this is often easier and faster to test and make changes before wasting time and resources into what could be a canceled idea or project. Prototyping may also take place during active development to test new ideas as the game emerges.

Prototypes are often meant only to act as a proof of concept or to test ideas, by adding, modifying or removing some of the features. Most algorithms and features debuted in a prototype may be ported to the game once they have been completed.

Often prototypes need to be developed quickly with very little time for up-front design (around 15 to 20 minutes of testing). Therefore, usually very prolific programmers are called upon to quickly code these testbed tools. RAD tools may be used to aid in the quick development of these programs. In case the prototype is in a physical form, programmers and designers alike will make the game with paper, dice, and other easy to access tools in order to make the prototype faster.

A successful development model is iterative prototyping, where design is refined based on current progress. There are various technology available for video game development.

## Production

Production is the main stage of development, when assets and source code for the game are produced.

Mainstream production is usually defined as the period of time when the project is fully staffed. Programmers write new source code, artists develop game assets, such as, sprites or 3D models. Sound engineers develop sound effects and composers develop music for the game. Level designers create levels, and writers write dialogue for cutscenes and NPCs. Game designers continue to develop the game's design throughout production.

## Design

Game design is an essential and collaborative process of designing the content and rules of a game, requiring artistic and technical competence as well as writing skills. Creativity and an open mind is vital for the completion of a successful video game.

During development, the game designer implements and modifies the game design to reflect the current vision of the game. Features and levels are often removed or added. The art treatment may evolve and the backstory may change. A new platform may be targeted as well as a new demographic. All these changes need to be documented and disseminated to the rest of the team. Most changes occur as updates to the design document.

## Programming

The programming of the game is handled by one or more game programmers. They develop prototypes to test ideas, many of which may never make it into the final game. The programmers incorporate new features demanded by the game design and fix any bugs introduced during the development process. Even if an off-the-shelf game engine is used, a great deal of programming is required to customize almost every game.

## Level Creation

From a time standpoint, the game's first level takes the longest to develop. As level designers and artists use the tools for level building, they request features and changes to the in-house tools that allow for quicker and higher quality development. Newly introduced features may cause old levels to become obsolete, so the levels developed early on may be repeatedly developed and discarded. Because of the dynamic environment of game development, the design of early levels may also change over time. It is not uncommon to spend upwards of twelve months on one level of a game developed over the course of three years. Later levels can be developed much more quickly as the feature set is more complete and the game vision is clearer and more stable.

## Art Production

## Audio Production

Game audio may be separated into three categories—sound effects, music, and voice-over.

Sound effect production is the production of sounds by either tweaking a sample to a desired effect or replicating it with real objects. Sound effects are important and impact the game's delivery.

Music may be synthesized or performed live.

There are several ways in which music is presented in a game.

- Music may be ambient, especially for slow periods of game, where the music aims to reinforce the aesthetic mood and game setting.

- Music may be triggered by in-game events. For example, in such games as Pac-Man or Mario, player picking up power-ups triggered respective musical scores.

- Action music, such as chase, battle or hunting sequences is fast-paced, hard-changing score.

- Menu music, similar to credits music, creates aural impact while relatively little action is taking place.

A game title with 20 hours of single-player gameplay may feature around 60 minutes of music.

Voice-overs and voice acting creates character gameplay interactivity. Voice acting adds personality to the game's characters.

## Testing

At the end of the project, quality assurance plays a significant role. Testers start work once anything is playable. This may be one level or subset of the game software that can be used to any reasonable extent. Early on, testing a game occupies a relatively small amount of time. Testers may work on several games at once. As development draws to a close, a single game usually employs many testers full-time (and often with overtime). They strive to test new features and regression test existing ones. Testing is vital for modern, complex games as single changes may lead to catastrophic consequences.

At this time features and levels are being finished at the highest rate and there is more new material to be tested than during any other time in the project. Testers need to carry out regression testing to make sure that features that have been in place for months still operate correctly. Regression testing is one of the vital tasks required for effective software development. As new features are added, subtle changes to the codebase can produce unexpected changes in different portions of the game. This task is often overlooked, for several reasons. Sometimes, when a feature is implemented and tested, it is considered "working" for the rest of the project and little attention is given to repeated testing. Also, features that are added late in development are prioritized and existing features often receive insufficient testing time. Proper regression testing is also increasingly expensive as the number of features increases and is often not scheduled correctly.

Despite the dangers of overlooking regression testing, some game developers and publishers fail to test the full feature suite of the game and ship a game with bugs. This can result in customers dissatisfaction and failure to meet sales goals. When this does happen, most developers and publishers quickly release patches that fix the bugs and make the game fully playable again.

## Milestones

Commercial game development projects may be required to meet milestones set by publisher. Milestones mark major events during game development and are used to track game's progress. Such milestones may be, for example, first playable, alpha, or beta game versions. Project milestones depend on the developer schedules.

Milestones are usually based on multiple short descriptions for functionality; examples may be "Player roaming around in game environment" or "Physics working, collisions, vehicle" etc. (numerous descriptions are possible). These milestones are usually how the developer gets paid; sometimes as "an advance against royalty". These milestones are listed, anywhere from three to twenty depending on developer and publisher. The milestone list is usually a collaborative agreement between the publisher and developer. The developer usually advocates for making the milestone descriptions as simple as possible; depending on the specific publisher - the milestone agreements may get very detailed for a specific game. When working with a good publisher, the "spirit of the law" is usually adhered to regarding milestone completion in other words if the milestone is 90% complete the milestone is usually paid with the understanding that it will be 100% complete by the next due milestone. It is a collaborative agreement between publisher and developer, and usually (but not always) the developer is constrained by heavy monthly development expenses that need to be met. Also, sometimes milestones are "swapped", the developer or publisher may mutually agree to amend the agreement and rearrange milestone goals depending on changing requirements and development resources available. Milestone agreements are usually included as part of the legal development contracts. After each "milestone" there is usually a payment arrangement. Some very established developers may simply have a milestone agreement based on the amount of time the game is in development (monthly / quarterly) and not specific game functionality - this is not as common as detailed functionality "milestone lists".

There is no industry standard for defining milestones, and such vary depending on publisher, year, or project. Some common milestones for two-year development cycle are as follows:

## First Playable

The first playable is the game version containing representative gameplay and assets, this is the first version with functional major gameplay elements. It is often based on the prototype created in pre-production. Alpha and first playable are sometimes used to refer to a single milestone, however large projects require first playable before feature complete alpha. First playable occurs 12 to 18 months before code release. It is sometimes referred to as the "Pre-Alpha" stage.

## Alpha

Alpha is the stage when key gameplay functionality is implemented, and assets are partially finished. A game in alpha is feature complete, that is, game is playable and contains all the major features. These features may be further revised based on testing and feedback. Additional small, new features may be added, similarly planned, but unimplemented features may be dropped. Programmers focus mainly on finishing the codebase, rather than implementing additions. Alpha occurs eight to ten months before code release, but this can vary significantly based on the scope of content and assets any given game has.

## Code freeze

Code freeze is the stage when new code is no longer added to the game and only bugs are being corrected. Code freeze occurs three to four months before code release.

## Beta

Beta is feature and asset complete version of the game, when only bugs are being fixed. This version contains no bugs that prevent the game from being shippable. No changes are made to the game features, assets, or code. Beta occurs two to three months before code release.

## Code Release

Code release is the stage when many bugs are fixed and game is ready to be shipped or submitted for console manufacturer review. This version is tested against QA test plan. First code release candidate is usually ready three to four weeks before code release.

## Gold Master

Gold master is the final game's build that is used as a master for production of the game.

## Crunch Time

Overtime is expected in the games industry. Particularly, crunch time or crunch mode is unpaid overtime requested by many companies to meet project deadlines and milestones that negatively affects game developers. A team missing a deadline risks the danger of having the project cancelled or employees being laid off. Although many companies are reducing the amount of crunch time, it is still prominent in smaller companies.

Many companies offer time-off, called comp time or extra paid time off after product ships to compensate for crunch time's negative effects. Some companies offer bonuses and financial rewards for successful milestone reach. Sometimes on-site crunch meals are offered and delivered to the team during crunch time.

The International Game Developers Association (IGDA) surveyed nearly 1,000 game developers in 2004 and produced a report to highlight the many problems caused by bad practice.

## Post-production

After the game goes gold and ships, some developers will give team members *comp time* (perhaps up to a week or two) to compensate for the overtime put in to complete the game, though this compensation is not standard.

## Maintenance

Once a game ships, the maintenance phase for the video game begins.

Games developed for video game consoles have had almost no maintenance period in the past. The shipped game would forever house as many bugs and features as when released. This was common for consoles since all consoles had identical or nearly identical hardware; making incompatibility, the cause of many bugs, a non-issue. In this case, maintenance would only occur in the case of a port, sequel, or enhanced remake that reuses a large portion of the engine and assets.

In recent times popularity of online console games has grown, and online capable video game consoles and online services such as Xbox Live for the Xbox have developed. Developers can maintain their software through downloadable patches. These changes would not have been possible in the past without the widespread availability of the Internet.

PC development is different. Game developers try to account for majority of configurations and hardware. However, the number of possible configurations of hardware and software inevitably leads to discovery of game-breaking circumstances that the programmers and testers didn't account for.

Programmers wait for a period to get as many bug reports as possible. Once the developer thinks they've obtained enough feedback, the programmers start working on a patch. The patch may take weeks or months to develop, but it's intended to fix most accounted bugs and problems with the game that were overlooked past code release, or in rare cases, fix unintended problems caused by previous patches. Occasionally a patch may include extra features or content or may even alter gameplay.

In the case of a massively multiplayer online game (MMOG), such as a MMORPG or MMORTS, the shipment of the game is the starting phase of maintenance. Such online games are in continuous maintenance as the gameworld is continuously changed and iterated and new features are added. The maintenance staff for a popular MMOG can number in the dozens, sometimes including members of the original programming team.

## Outsourcing

Several development disciplines, such as audio, dialogue, or motion capture, occur for relatively short periods of time. Efficient employment of these roles requires either large development house with multiple simultaneous title production or outsourcing from third-party vendors. Employing personnel for these tasks full-time is expensive, so a majority of developers outsource a portion of the work. Outsourcing plans are conceived during the pre-production stage; where the time and finances required for outsourced work are estimated.

- The music cost ranges based on length of composition, method of performance (live or synthesized), and composer experience. In 2003 a minute of high quality synthesized music cost between US$600-1.5k. A title with 20 hours of gameplay and 60 minutes of music may have cost $50k-60k for its musical score.

- Voice acting is well-suited for outsourcing as it requires a set of specialized skills. Only large publishers employ in-house voice actors.

- Sound effects can also be outsourced.

- Programming is generally outsourced less than other disciplines, such as art or music. However, outsourcing for extra programming work or savings in salaries has become more common in recent years.

## Marketing

The game production has similar distribution methods to those of music and film industries.

The publisher's marketing team targets the game for a specific market and then advertises it. The team advises the developer on target demographics and market trends, as well as suggests specific features. The game is then advertised and the game's high concept is incorporated into the promotional material, ranging from magazine ads to TV spots. Communication between developer and marketing is important.

The length and purpose of a game demo depends on the purpose of the demo and target audience. A game's demo may range between a few seconds (such as clips or screenshots) to hours of gameplay. The demo is usually intended for journalists, buyers, trade shows, general public, or internal employees (who, for example, may need to familiarize with the game to promote it). Demos are produced with public relations, marketing and sales in mind, maximizing the presentation effectiveness.

## Trade Show Demo

As a game nears completion, the publisher will want to showcase a demo of the title at trade shows. Many games have a "Trade Show demo" scheduled.

The major annual trade shows are, for example, Electronic Entertainment Expo (E3) or Penny Arcade Expo (PAX). E3 is the largest show in North America. E3 is hosted primarily for marketing and business deals. New games and platforms are announced at E3 and it received broad press coverage. Thousands of products are on display and press demonstration schedules are kept. In recent years E3 has become a more closed-door event and many advertisers have withdrawn, reducing E3's budget. PAX, created by authors of Penny Arcade blog and web-comic, is a mature and playful event with a player-centred philosophy.

## Localization

A game created in one language may also be published in other countries which speak a different language. For that region, the game needs to be translated for the game to be playable. For example, some games created for PlayStation Vita were initially published in Japanese language, like Soul Sacrifice. Non-native speakers of the game's original language may have to wait for translation of the game to their language. But most modern big-budget games take localization into account during the development process and the games are released for several different languages simultaneously.

Localization is the actual process of translating the language assets in a game into other languages. By localizing games, they increase their level of accessibility where games could help to expend the international markets effectively. Game localization is generally known as language translations yet a "full localization" of a game is a complex project. Different levels of translation range from: zero translation being that there is no translation to the product and all things are sent raw, basic translation where only a few text and subtitles are translated or even added, and a full translation where new voice overs and game material changes are added.

There are various essential elements on localizing a game including translating the language of the game to adjusting in-game assets for different cultures to reach more potential consumers in other geographies (or globalization for short). Translation seems to fall into scope of localization, which itself constitutes a substantially broader endeavor. These include the different levels of translation to the globalization of the game itself. However, certain developers seem to be divided on whether globalization falls under localization or not.

Moreover, in order to fit into the local markets, game production companies often change or re-design the graphic designs or the packaging of the game for marketing purposes. For example, the popular game *Assassin's Creed* has two different packaging designs for the Japanese and US market. By localizing the graphic and packaging designs, companies might arouse a better connections and attention from the consumers from various regions.

## Video Game Developer

Video game developers, also known as games developers or video game programmers, write code for games for a variety of formats, such as PCs, consoles, web browsers and mobile phones. They take the video game designer's ideas, drawings and rules, and turn them into a playable game with visuals and sound through writing code.

The work of a games developer typically involves:

- Looking at the design specifications of video game designers.
- Writing code to turn the designer's concepts into a playable game.
- Using application program interfaces (APIs) – a set of pre-built commands that allow different softwares to interact.
- Programming the game's terrain.
- Programming artificial intelligence for non-player characters within the game.

## How to Become Video Game Developer

Game programming is a field that keeps on growing by leaps and bounds. However, both the job itself and the path to it can be pretty grueling, so before you embark on it, it's important to consider whether it's the right decision for you. If it is, acquiring the necessary skills is a must, since employers are looking for know-how and rarely, if ever, offer on-the-job training. Once you're equipped with those, patience and perseverance definitely help when you finally go on the job hunt.

### Method 1. Learning How to Program

1. Decide between school and self-taught. Expect employers to value technical know-how most of all. So don't fret if the cost of tuition for higher education is beyond your means, because a degree

isn't strictly necessary to find employment. At the same time, though, recognize that technical proficiency coupled with a degree will probably make you stand out over other candidates.

- Whichever route you choose, put all your emphasis on becoming a proficient programmer. Coasting will only leave you ill-equipped for interviews and the job in question.

2. Choose your major carefully. If you decide on college, be wary about specialized degrees in game programming. Expect these to cover all of the many different aspects of game programming in a relatively short amount of time. Favor a major in Computer Science instead if you aren't already proficient in the subject.

- Each aspect of game programming takes a lot of time to master. Studying computer science in depth is more likely to equip you with the necessary skills to tackle each one, even if those skills aren't directly applied to games during the course of your studies.

- If you do consider a specialized degree, research the people who are teaching it. Professors who understand the concepts of game programming, but who have never worked in the field themselves, may not be the best people to learn from.

3. Learn computer languages. Whether you go to school or teach yourself, aim to master at least one computer language. Focus on C++ to increase your chances of being hired, since this is used the most often in game programming. Other languages that are helpful include:

- Actionscript
- Assembly
- C

- Java
- Objective-C
- Python
- Swift

4. Design your own game. Remember: the best way to learn how to do something is to actually do it. Once you learn how to code in computer languages, apply your skills. Build a game from the ground up to grow more familiar with the whole process, from start to finish. As you do, you should:

- Keep it basic. Don't worry about revolutionizing games as you know it. To make an analogy, write a simple short story, not James Joyce's *Ulysses*.

- Copy another game if needed. The purpose here is to learn, not to be original. Borrow another game's concept and build on it if you're stuck for ideas.

- Do everything yourself. Don't rely on using outside vector/math libraries. Make all aspects a DIY project in order to increase your proficiency.

- Finish it. You want to grow familiar with the whole process, so follow through all the way to the end. Don't abandon it just because you've already finished your favorite aspect of programming.

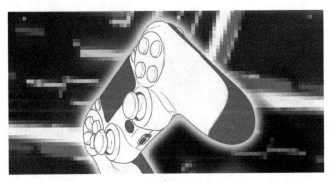

5. Narrow down your focus. Remember: as a professional game developer, you'll be part of a team tasked with specific aspects. So as you learn to code and build your own games, decide on which areas you want to concentrate on when hired. Once you do, continue to work on personal projects and place more attention to these areas.

- Titles and departments may vary from company to company, but generally programming is divided between: artificial intelligence; animation; audio; build systems; engines; gameplay; networking; physics; rendering; tools; and user interface.

## Method 2. Finding Work

1. Intern first. Before you apply for a paid position, put in some time with an unpaid one. Search online or through your school for open internships. Gain working experience to bolster your resume when it comes time for the job hunt. Other benefits of an internship include:

- References from industry insiders.

- Extended contacts with people in the field.

- More familiarity with the day-to-day reality of the job.

2. Have demos ready. Since you don't have any published games to point to, prepare some examples on your own to submit along with your cover letter and resume. Continue developing personal projects and publish them online in a public Git repository where employers can check them out. Don't worry about creating whole games. Instead, develop short-and-sweet demos that highlight the specific areas that you want to specialize in.

- Whatever your demo might be, make it perfect. Don't try to wow interviewers with something overly complex if you can't get it right. Showcase something simple and flawless instead.

3. Focus on start-ups at first. This isn't to say that you shouldn't apply to positions with established, well-known, successful companies. However, such companies are better situated to offer higher pay and possibly more job security, so expect your competition here to be pretty fierce. Concentrate instead on newer, smaller companies, who, like you, probably have to be less choosy.

- This isn't a guarantee that you'll get hired, but you're less likely to be up against programming rockstars with way more experience than you.

4. Research each company you apply to. First of all, look for job postings on company websites. Then, after you submit an application, brush up on the company. Read their own published profile, as well as any write-ups from outside sources. Jot down any questions that occur to you so you can pose them in your interview.

- In addition to your technical skills, demonstrating a working knowledge of both the company and the game business at large in your interview should raise your standing among other candidates.

5. Network. Expect to face a lot of competition for each position. Use each and every personal

connection that you have with industry insiders to get a step ahead. Find out about potential openings before they're posted. Ask your contacts to provide recommendations if they have an inside track with employers. Extend your network by:

- Reaching out through online forums, social media, and professional networks to meet people in the field.

- Staying in frequent contact with current or former classmates and professors.

- Attending conferences and conventions.

6. Make the most of failed interviews. First of all, keep in mind that with so much competition, you'll probably face a lot of rejection. Accept it as a given, take it in stride, and learn from it by:

- Reflecting on your interviews, resume, and demos to identify and improve weak points.

- Following up with a thank-you letter or email to interviewers for being considered at all.

- Asking for pointers on areas in which they think you need improvement.

## Method 3. Deciding if this Career is Right for you

1. Love games. Keep in mind that programming can be a demanding and stressful field to work in,

as well as a difficult career to break into. It will require a lot of passion on your part, so take stock of just how much you have. Muster up every last drop that you can in order to succeed.

2. Expect a long road ahead of you. Value patience and persistence. Plan on taking a few years to acquire the necessary technical know-how, either on your own or through formal education. Then, when you're ready to enter the workforce, expect a lot of competition for each opening, which means it might take a while to find work. Then, once hired, anticipate having to do a lot of grunt work before advancing to your desired position.

3. Don't do it for the money. If you go the formal education route, bear in mind that its cost will probably exceed a game programmer's average yearly salary by a pretty hefty amount. Also keep in mind that the field lacks job security, which means you may have gaps in your employment. Again, this career definitely requires you to be passionate about it, so do it for the love, not a quick buck.

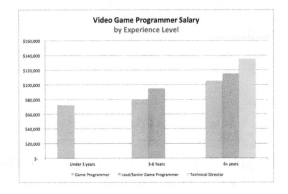

4. Anticipate a heavy emphasis on math. Expect most, if not all, aspects of game programming to require strong math skills. If you're still in school, double down on your math courses. If you're out of school and need to brush up, definitely do so.

- Obviously, taking math courses is a great way to strengthen your skills. But perhaps even better for the aspiring game developer are the multitude of math games available for download. Kill two birds with one stone and explore games that you may not have otherwise sampled.

5. Be a team player. Before you enter the field professionally, you should spend a lot of time developing programming skills on your own. But don't grow too accustomed to working solo. Once hired, expect to become one member of a much larger team. Prioritize clear communication and the ability to accept criticism as two essential skillsets.

6. Be flexible about location. Depending on where you live, this may not be as much of an issue. But if your hometown isn't already a booming tech haven, be willing to move to where the work is. Also remember that job stability is pretty iffy, which means you may have to relocate again for a new job.

## How to Become a Video Game Programmer

Video games are extremely popular amongst adults as well as children. Many of them are so very engrossed and fascinated with the game that they want to learn to program it on their own. Another attraction about learning video game programming is that it can be a lucrative career. If your game is a success you can be a millionaire. In case you too have developed a die-hard passion for this tech game so much so that you want to become a video game programmer yourself, here are some instructions on how you can make your own video game. If you are sincere and hard working, you definitely can learn video game programming. Keep confidence in yourself.

## Steps

1. Be informed: Talk to your peers, senior, visit campuses or read online and offline magazines on video game programming such as 'Gamasutra' or 'Gameslice' to get a knack of the field you are considering to enter. Also find out what training and skills are a must if you wish to become a pro in the field.

2. Know where your skills lie: Video game programming has grown enormous in size, it is kind of becoming something like movie-making where different set of professionals are required to make the perfect picture. Video game productions involves level designers to make it more fun, programmers to write the source-code and scripts, 3D modelers to craft the player and artists to design the box and advertising materials. Know where your specialization lies and take a course accordingly.

3. Get yourself the desired training: If you are serious about learning video game design invest in a

training course that offers hands-on training on video game production. These days, you can also enroll yourself for online courses in schools such as UAT Online Game Degree and DeVry University.

4. Get friendly with commercially available game engines: Commercially available game engines like 'Cry Engine', 'Radiant', 'Source' and 'Unreal' Engine come along with the games. These let you create your own characters, levels and maps. You can take help of video tutorials and online documents to learn how to work on these game engines.

5. Learn programming: This is fundamental if you want to pursue video game programming professionally. Knowledge of programming languages such as C++, one of the most popular language used in gaming is a must to understand the intricacies of video game programming. If you are beginning, consider taking a course in 'DarkBASIC', this language is highly recommended for the programming beginners. You can also consider taking a course in Microsoft Visual Basic that teaches you to learn programming for Windows operating systems.

6. Adapt problem-solving attitude: Video game programming requires good degree of patience

and perseverance. You'll encounter several problems; you should develop an attitude to solve these problems in a calm and composed manner.

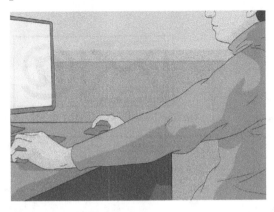

7. Practice as much as you can: Video game programming cannot be learnt in a jiffy. Do practice as much as possible to get into the programming mode. Start with basic level games and then move on when you achieve perfection in that level. Take help of books, online tutorials to develop your skill and achieve mastery in programming.

8. Learn to make your own video game in summer camps: These days, several summer camps are organized that teach you video game design and video game programming. So you can also get some summer learning on video game programming as well.

9. Contact the right people. Try to look for local programmers in your area. If you do not know any local programmers, try to contact these programmers that are able to help.

10. -declancarpenter01@gmail.com [Willing to help people that wish to learn how to create 2D games].

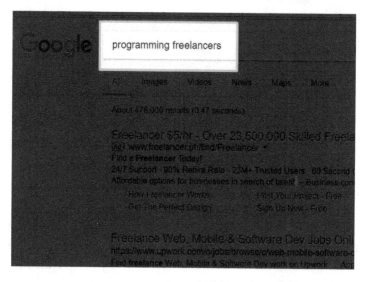

11. If this doesn't work, try searching Google for programming freelancers.

## How to Become an Artist for Video Games

In the past twenty years, video games have evolved from relatively simple screen representations to complex 3-dimensional worlds where the characters seem to leap off the screen. Along with more complex imagery, the job of video game artist has evolved into a number of different roles, each with its own distinct tasks: concept artist, 2-D animator, 3-D animator, and 2-D texture artist. You'll need to understand all of these different roles before choosing your area of expertise and becoming an artist for video games. Read the following steps to find out how to become an artist for video games.

## Steps

1. Learn all you can about character animation and video games. This includes going back to the very first Disney cartoons and studying how animation and characters have evolved over the years into the Manga, Anime, and other lifelike characters featured in video games.

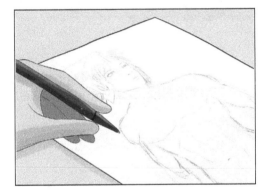

2. Draw incessantly. The best way to learn how to draw is to do it.

You can take classes at a local art school to develop your skills, but you can also teach yourself through observation, reading and practice.

- It's a good idea to study anatomy and exterior settings so you understand the basics before trying to animate them, as every animation starts with a sketch, which is then scanned into the computer and developed in Photoshop before going through the animation process.

3. Get a bachelors or associates degree, or a certificate, in a video games related field. For exam-

ple, many universities in the United States, such as the Massachusetts Institute of Technology (MIT), are now offering video game courses as part of comparative media studies or software engineering.

4. Learn computer graphics skills.

- Adobe Photoshop and Illustrator are essential 2-D programs to develop characters, while 3ds Max and Maya are some of the most popular 3-D modeling programs.

- You can teach yourself by means of tutorials from sites such as Computer Arts, or you can take courses to learn how to use the software. There are also animation certificate programs that last between 6 months and 2 years.

5. Determine what part of video game design you enjoy most.

- A concept artist comes up with original ideas for settings and characters.

- A 2-D animator takes the concept artist's sketches and creates 2-dimensional animation from them.

- A 3-D animator takes the work a step further and adds the modeling and building to create 3-D animations.

- A 2-D texture artist creates all of the different textures used in a video game, from the hairs on a characters head to the scales on a reptilian character.

6. Choose your specialty and create a portfolio of your best work. Your portfolio should consist of a number of different designs or creations, and if possible, demonstrate their use in video games. You can save your files on a CD-ROM, a website, or both, so long as you can provide potential employers with samples of your work upon request.

7. Apply for an internship with an animation studio. This will allow you to learn the entire process of creating animations for video games, from concept to interface design.

- Most companies that develop video games are in Austin, Boston, Los Angeles, San Francisco, Seattle, North Carolina, and Washington D.C.

- You can look for both jobs and internships on job portals like Monsterboard, but you can also look on the websites of video game companies themselves. In addition, you can use your social network to find out about current openings.

8. Apply for a job as a video game artist, either at the company where you interned, or at another company. Make sure your resume and portfolio reflect your strengths and showcase your talent by highlighting any video games you've worke d on - even if they are non-professional - and including references if you have any.

# Processes of Video Game Development

Video game development is a software development process. Game development involves an integration of agile development and Personal Software Process (PSP). Several pre-production, production and post-production processes are involved. The topics elaborated in this chapter cover the various processes of video game development such as programming a video game, designing a successful platforming game, making a simple PC video game, coding video game, making a video game side quest, etc.

## How to Develop a Game

Generally, a game must include creative backgrounds, thriller plot, immense graphics, and super sound. These steps will show you how to effectively plan your game content development project, staff your game development team, and will walk you through all stages from idea development to product finalization and release.

**Steps**

1. Make sure you think your game idea through to its end in order to have a complete vision of your end product.

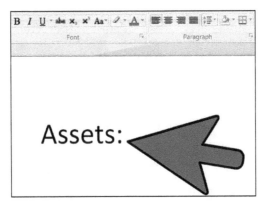

2. Create a list of all assets you need to create vs the timeframe of their completion in order to make

the right decision about your future development team structure and skills needed to develop a game.

3. Consult with a gaming industry expert or those who understand game development process to get insights and gather feedback on your game idea (basically, try to get expert answers to such questions as "is it still topical?", "what do other similar games offer?", "how will my game make a difference?")

## Method 1. Work on the Game Plot Development

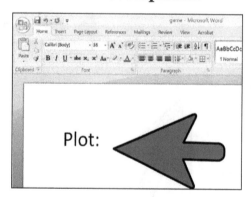

1. Have a story. Game plot is needed to push the action along. The plot will help you determine the type of assets you will need to develop the actual game.

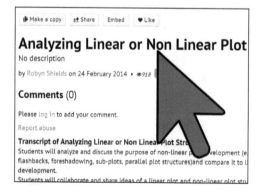

2. Develop your game's plot in a narrative way, just as if you were writing a fiction story. You may use linear or non-linear plot development.

3. When you've developed a plot, try to draft out how your players will be exposed to the plot during the gameplay .

## Method 2. Building a Development Team

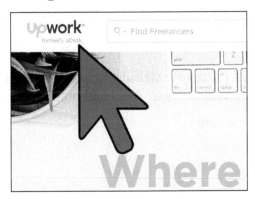

1. Determine the skills that will most likely be needed for your game development project. Due to the cost factor, many startup game studios make a common critical mistake – they hire few specialists to fulfill several roles. As a rule, these specialists are pretty junior and are managed by a single senior guy. Such team structures often fail to deliver quality products on time because of occupational burnout (having to work overtime to meet the deadlines, multi-tasking, etc) and lack of professional expertise.

2. Hire mid and senior IT and creative guys for the most complex tasks within your game development project and have one person do his own work.

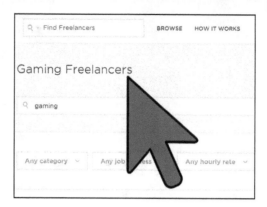

3. Consider your hiring options. Since timing and cost efficiency are really two most important factors in gaining a competitive advantage and winning a certain market or a niche, you should consider alternative ways to staff your game development project (e.g., offshore IT staffing, Dedicated Development Team, etc.).

    a. For your game development project you'll need these skills and roles (as a minimum):

- Concept artist:
    1. Preparation of all creative materials including sketches, drafts, creation of characters, objects (e.g., vehicles, weapons) and map layouts,
    2. 2D / 3D artwork creation,
    3. Basic design.

- Level designer:
    1. Knowledge of 3d party design tools such as UnrealEd and 3D art packages (Max/Maya),
    2. 2D / 3D modeling,
    3. Game mapping.

- Modeler:
    1. Conversion of 2D artwork into 3D assets to be imported into your game,
    2. Polygonal modeling.

- Animator:
    1. Creation of control systems to turn your character models into the digital puppets to manipulate with,
    2. Creation of the entire game's motion system.

- Software developer:
    1. Coding and integrating the whole functionality into the game,
    2. Front-end and back-end programming.

- Project Manager (or Team Lead):

  1. Oversees the project and makes sure each project element is completed on time and on budget,

  2. Helps unite the team, solve internal problems, increase team morale,

  3. Acts as an intermediary between client and game development service provider.

- Web designer:

  1. Creation of game's webpages, online communities and other online media outlets used to promote your game,

  2. Keeping all web properties' design up to date.

- QA Engineer:

  1. Oversees the project from the quality's perspective,

  2. Checks the game for bugs and errors,

  3. Conducts full quality assurance control.

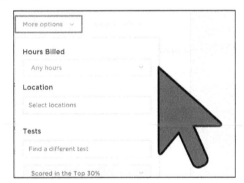

4. Schedule your Game Production.

- Create an individual schedule for each team member stating specific details and timeframes for each task assigned to the person.

- Compile all of the individual schedules into a Master Schedule and build your Agile Scrum practice around it.

5. Work on the Game production.

- After production has officially kicked off, make sure:

  1. Your PM / team lead follows both the team as a whole and each individual team member's progress and keeps everyone on schedule,

  2. Your PM / team lead only uses constructive rather than destructive criticism to maintain a healthy team morale,

  3. Your PM / team lead is able to minimize (inevitable) delays in the delivery

- Game development stages:

  1. Integrating all completed project assets into a functional game (level designers and developers are mostly involved here),

  2. Alpha and Beta testing and feedback collection,

  3. Remodeling and finalizing,

  4. Releasing your game to the app stores and game centers

## How to Design a Video Game

Now is pretty much the best time there's ever been to be a game developer. The market is extremely open to newcomers and people are playing more games than ever. But if you're not already knee-deep in the industry, it can be confusing. It's like entering a dungeon without a map and compass. Below, we discuss what you'll have to design to create a complete game, give some basic pro tips on how to do it well, and show you what to do to take your career and game pro.

### Part 1. Designing Gameplay

1. Determine your goals. What are you trying to do with this game? What story are you trying to tell? What do you want your players to feel at the end? What kind of experience do you want it to be? What do you want to get out of the project? These are some important questions you'll need to ask yourself before you begin the process, because the answers will provide the light at the end of the tunnel for this process. You need to know where you're going if you want to get there efficiently.

2. Determine your audience. Different audiences are more likely to play in different ways. They are also more likely to prefer different types of games and have different standards for content. Remember, it's fine to want to make a game for a very specific audience, but it will limit the profits that you make. Be realistic.

3. Design for different devices. Before you get very far into the process, you need to consider what kind of devices you want your game to be on. Mobile platforms are quickly becoming a major player but PC and consoles are still (and will likely remain) strong. The programming involved, and especially the interface and controls, will change drastically with your platform, so it's important to understand what you're going to be putting the game on.

4. Consider your genre. While genres are not completely important, the genre of your game will determine some parts of how it's designed. Is it an FPS? A platformer? An RPG? A social game?

There are very few aspects of design that are not influenced by the genre. Of course, you can say "forget genres" and just make whatever you want, but this is more difficult to market and you will be forced to be more creative and original: not the easiest way to break into the design world.

- One of the things that you'll have to think about when designing based on genre is how you want the UI to look. Different types of games will have the UI more or less visible, depending usually upon the complexity of controls.

- Another consideration is that while some genres lack it almost entirely, other game genres have become synonymous with dialogue. Will your dialogue need to be recorded? Will you do it text based? How interactive will it be? Planning ahead for dialogue is important, as you'll have to not only design the system itself but also the dialogue trees.

- You'll need to decided on a combat system for many types of games, or find the equivalent if your game does not have combat. Think of this as the "game" part of the game. It is arguably one of the most important parts of design and having a model to work from is very helpful.

5. Determine player agency options. As a general rule, you want your players to feel like they have a choice in what they're doing. However, certain types of games have come to be associated with much more choice than others. Adding choices can be very complex but it can also be relatively simple, depending on how you decide to do it.

- Some games give the appearance of having choice, for example, but actually have very little choice involved. This can be done well or it can be done poorly.

- An example of choice done well would be the Bioshock series or Witcher 2. An example of choices done poorly would be something like Old Republic.

6. Outline your challenges. The serious design work begins next: you need to create your gameplay

loop. This is an outline of how your game works. It usually ends with your player's goal and details the challenges they'll have and the goals they'll need to meet. An example would be the first Mario game, where the loop would look like: run, avoid obstacles, hit flagpole.

7. Create the incentives for your player. No matter what kind of game you're making, you need to give your player a good reason to want to achieve the goals and progress through the whole game. It needs to be proportionately rewarding for the level of the challenge it poses. One great way to do that is by locking levels until you have completed them, that way you feel like you are getting an incentive.

8. Balance difficulty with playability. You also need to make sure that the game isn't too hard, or at least not so hard that it makes playing the game impossible or nearly impossible. Your game should pose some challenge, but not so much that it's going to induce a lot of rage quit. This usually requires some testing, but that's okay: that's what betas are for.

## Part 2. Covering the Components

1. Design the tutorial. There are many different ways to do the tutorial and many different philosophies

about the best way to go about it. You can hide the tutorial within a story about the player character getting training (aka Fable), or you can simply display instructions (aka Mass Effect). You can even try to hide the tutorial altogether blending it seamlessly into the game or display all of the tutorial all at once. No matter what you do, make sure that it feels natural within your game.

2. Design the world. The world is the environments in which your player will play the game. How expansive will your world be? How challenging? How will you indicate that an area should be explored? That it shouldn't? These are things you'll need to consider.

3. Design the mechanics. These are the internal rules of the game. You'll want to decide on a rule system and make sure that it's balanced and consistent. The best way to do this is to look at what other games do right or wrong in this area.

4. Design your levels. The levels are the individual chunks of the game, the "episodes" that the

player has to get through to make it to the end of the game. The levels should be engaging and just the right amount of challenging. They should also be physically laid out in a way that makes sense.

5. Design the content. You'll need to design all the content, like the items that can be interacted with, the characters themselves, the environmental items, etc. This can be extremely time consuming so plan ahead. Try to find clever ways to recycle things without making them seem repetitive.

6. Design the interface. The interface includes things like the menus and UI. You want these to be easy to navigate and natural to use. Take cues from your favorite games but remember that generally the simpler the better. If an 8-year-old can figure it out, you're set.

7. Design the controls. Having controls which feel natural are key to players really enjoying and

getting the most out of your game. Remember to keep things simple and streamlined. When in doubt, conform to standardized control systems.

## Part 3. Designing Visuals

1. Make your visuals match your game. The way your game looks should match the type of game that you're making. Peppy, colorful graphics, for example, can ruin a game meant to have a serious tone. You also want to avoid pixel like 8-bit style if making a game that is meant to come across as modern.

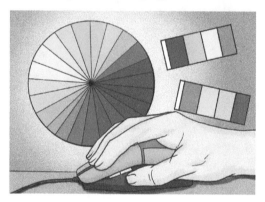

2. Choose a cohesive, appealing color palette. Charming visuals are an important part of making a game. Bad ones can kill a players enjoyment of the game. Read up on some color theory and, as with most things, remember that when in doubt: take the simple route.

3. Use visual significance. You can play on cliches to help make your game easier to navigate and play. Use commonly accepted icons and visual cues to keep your player immersed in the world. You can

also use visuals to lead your players through a map, by making areas where you don't want them to go look , for example, dark and scary, but areas where you do want them to go clearly lit and interesting.

4. Don't feel limited to fancy graphics. Don't feel like you have to make the next Mass Effect to be a successful game maker. Visually simple games can be just as good if the game itself is good. An excellent example of this is Journey or Bastion, which had uncomplicated graphics but were both highly regarded.

## Part 4. Designing the Audio

1. Create your direct sound effects. Direct sound effects are things like voices, weapons noises, and item interaction sound effects. You'll want to make sure you have these in and that they make sense within your game. Try to get as many unique ones as possible, since too many of the same makes your game sound repetitive (giving you a bad case of "Then I Took an Arrow to The Knee" syndrome).

2. Create your ambient sound effects. Ambient sound effects are background noises, usually environmental. These are important as they help set the scene and make your players feel immersed in the game, so don't neglect them.

3. Try to use original work. When you're doing the sound work, it's a good idea to try to record as much original sound as possible. You can use a sample library, but people that know what they're doing will notice and it will come across as unprofessional.

4. Don't neglect your soundtrack. Music is also important to the game and you shouldn't forget about it. Sometimes, a soundtrack is all that's necessary to make a game really stand out, even if it's otherwise an unknown. Hire someone that knows what they're doing and use your soundtrack to help create an immersive player experience.

## Part 5. Designing your Story

1. Start with a solid concept. A bad concept is one of the things that can really kill a game, so it's important to have this really nailed down before you get too far. Think your concept all the

way through and be sure that it's complex enough to make for a rich world, characters, and gameplay.

2. Tailor your pacing. Pacing is the speed and intensity with which the plot or game itself comes at the player. Like with a good movie or book, you want the pacing of your game to be spot on. You don't want it to start really intense, for example, and then have the rest of the game feel comparatively boring. Generally the best pacing is to have an overall build to an intense climax, with the build make up of peaks and valleys of excitement and rest.

3. Learn about classic story telling techniques. Many of the best games make use of classic storytelling techniques. You should study these and see if they can help you in creating your game.

- Act structures are commonly used in plays, movies, and books to help get the pacing correct. Look up act structures if you're feeling unsure about your pacing.

- Monomyth or the Hero's Journey is one of the most common story-telling philosophies, arguing that most stories conform to an overall pattern. You can exploit this pattern to help it play on inherent human psychology. Journey is one of the best examples of the use of monomyth in games, but it can be found in most of them.

4. Avoid tropes. Tropes are storytelling cliches. Some are better than others and some can even be useful, but generally you should avoid as many cliches as possible. Spend a little time on the TVTropes website and see if you're designing a walking cliché.

## Part 6. Designing your Characters

1. Fully develop your characters. You want your characters to be full and rich, since this makes your players more engaged and invested in the game. This means giving characters complex personalities and faults. If you need help imagining and writing complex personalities, try some character development exercises, by plotting your character on the Myers-Briggs personality chart or the character alignment chart.

2. Leave room for character development. Your characters should change as people over the course of the game. This makes them more interesting. This means that they should generally start off with some major flaws or a generally worse personality than how they end up.

3. Get in your character's head. It's really easy when writing characters to make them do what we would do instead of what they would do. But this kind of lazy writing is often visible to players because it comes across as so unnatural. Focus on what your characters would do and you'll make your game much better.

4. Consider some diversity. Games tend to lack diversity, with characters being vastly more similar than in real life. This can make games feel similar and boring. By including diversity in your game, you can not only make it more interesting, but also increase the hype for your game by setting it apart from others.

## Part 7. Going Pro

1. Learn the skills you'll need. You'll need some skills in order to make a game (skills we can't teach you here because they are too complex). You might need to go to school in order to learn these skills

but it is technically possible to learn them on your own as well. You'll need a good understanding of math, since many games boil down to a series of equations. You'll also need to learn a programming language (usually C, C++, or C#). There are schools for game design, but your best bet is to go to the best school you can get into for programming. This will give you a more diverse skill set so that you can take a general job as a programmer if you don't immediately get hired with a company.

2. Start by making a small game. If you want to break into the industry and start working with major publishers, it's a good idea to start by just making a small but engaging game that shows your skills but doesn't require 5 years to make. This can get someone interested enough to give you a job or give you money. You also just don't want to bite off more than you can chew.

3. Stay indie. You don't need to get your game published by a major publisher. You don't have to be recognized by anyone but your players if you don't want to. The indie game market is alive and kicking and right now is the best time to be making this kind of game. Keep this in mind before strongly pursuing official backing.

4. Make use of Kickstarter and other crowd-funding sites. If you want to make a great game, of

any type at all, you're going to have to get some money. It takes a LOT of money to make a game. Currently, the best way to get that money is to run Kickstarter, which is one of many crowd-funding platforms. Check out some Kickstarters that have been successful in the past to see what they did right, but the main pieces of advice are to have great incentives and communicate constantly.

5. Get your game on Steam. Steam is Valve's digital game store and one of the most popular distribution channels for PC games. They are also one of the most friendly distribution channels for indie games. If you're making this type of game, your best bet for success is to get it on Steam. Currently, Steam Greenlight is the channel you will probably have to go through.

6. Build a fanbase. Build a website and an army of social media accounts for your game. Update constantly and let people feel involved in the process. Communicate as much as possible with people who become interested in what you're doing. Having people excited about your game is key to indie success, since interest is often the main factor in things like getting on Steam.

7. Make friends in the community. The indie community is very tight knit and many of them can

help you on your road to success. If you want to succeed, it's a good idea to make friends with them, help support them in their ventures, and promote their games. They'll help you do the same if they think you've got something worthwhile.

## How to Design a Successful Platforming Game

So you like playing Mario games? You want to design a platforming masterpiece of your own? Here are some useful rules for creating platforms that will entice players to play more (instead of frustrating them).

### Steps

1. Look before you jump. In real life, you wouldn't want to jump off a cliff without checking for a safe place to land. Similarly, your game shouldn't require the player to jump to a platform that can't be seen onscreen. That doesn't mean you can't surprise the player; just avoid "leaps of faith."

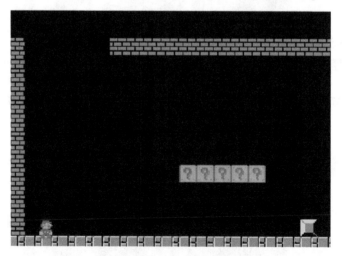

2. Keep it possible. At no point should it be impossible to complete a level. If you want the player to fall into a "trap," make it possible to continue the level (without perishing.). That means no inescapable obstacles or enemies that can't be defeated.

3. Use strategic energy placement. Put enemies in places that fit the level design and add to the challenge in a specific way. It might seem tempting to put a bunch of enemies in one place, but don't - it's been done way too many times already. Instead, use enemies in clever ways, or to create a puzzle for the player to solve.

4. Don't be arbitrary. Don't put coins or bonus items in places that can't be reached or that lead the player to an inevitable death. The player should be able to theoretically collect every power-up in the level, even if it is difficult to do so. So don't put doors, coins or power-ups in arbitrary places - it will only make the player frustrated.

## How to make a Simple PC Video Game

The main point of most homes around the world - some people often have a room just for gaming. If you like video games, why don't you make a simple one to begin with? This topic will help you make a simple video game for PC easily.

**Steps**

1. Figure out what program you want to use. One program is RPG Maker VX. This program isn't

free but you may wish to use the 2003 version - it's free. Some simple video games may also use coding, instead of point-and-click systems. A good basic coding is Python GUI which is free and open-source from their website.

2. Install your program and gather your ideas up ready. Surely you have a rough idea about what this game is about? If not, think about your favourite games, what games sell or simply think about fantasy. Fantasy is always a good starting point for (ok) game makers/designers. Mainly due to the fact about 96.23% of games are indeed fantasy [Fable, Dragon Age, WoW and even Kameo et cetera].

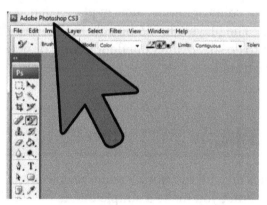

3. If needed [for people who know what game they want to make] you should make new foes or people to play as or kill. Use Photoshop, Gimp or even Window's basic Paint tool.

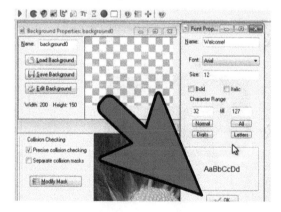

4. Now make your first map or level. Have an introductory page where you name and edit your

game character. The first map is usually plain and simple, don't go overboard on your first map.

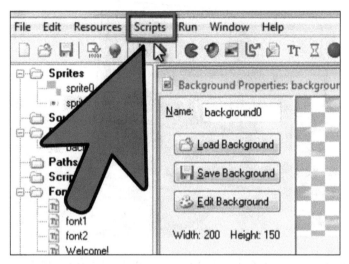

5. Make more levels. If you are more adept with game design then why not try your hand at scripting? This is however, harder to do and is really not advised to new designers. Also, you really should have a, well, a point. This makes a game a game. Maybe the point of a mini game is to kill the boss via doing a quest and then going to the boss.

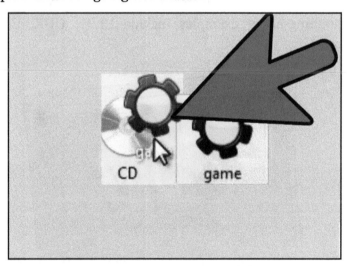

6. Make a game and pop it onto disk. Don't forget the credits.

## How to Program a Video Game

Phones, browsers, computers, consoles: video games are more popular and widespread than ever before. You can find more tutorials, asset collections, game-making software tools, and expert advice than ever before. Programming your own game still demands skill and patience, but there are enough resources for a coder of any level.

**Part 1. Getting Started**

1. Consider a game engine. Few game developers reinvent the wheel and write their own game engine from scratch, especially for their first game. If you want to dive right in, but still have plenty of opportunities for programming, using a game engine is a good option. An engine typically includes higher-level tools for altering 3D models, scripting events, and other common game applications, but will still provide plenty of hands-on programming opportunities.

- Popular programming-heavy examples include Unity, UDK, Unreal Engine 4, and CryENGINE.

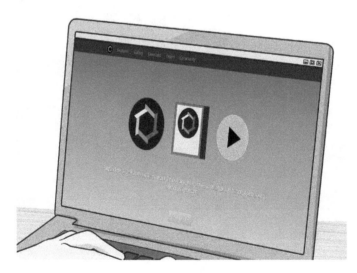

2. Use frameworks and other tools. A framework is a step below a game engine, but still provides a set of tools and APIs (application program interfaces) to save you time and streamline your coding projects. Consider this the minimum level of software to use for your first gaming project, and even then you should feel comfortable introducing yourself as a programmer, or have a deep interest in the behind-the-scenes work on game engines. Depending on the exact framework and/or game engine you are using, you may want to do some of the work in additional, specialized APIs, such as the popular OpenGL for creating 3D graphics.

- Polycode, Turbulenz, and MonoGame are example of frameworks created with both 2D and 3D games in mind.

3. Try an IDE. An Integrated Development Environment is a general-purpose compiler and collection of source files that makes complex programming projects easier to build. An IDE will make programming a game much more convenient, especially if it comes with built-in ways to interact with graphics and audio systems.

- Visual Studio and Eclipse are two examples, but there are many others. Look for an IDE based around a language you are familiar with.

4. Learn a programming language. Most of the tools above are based in a popular programming language, so following the accompanying tutorials will give you a great start. While you can create a game in almost any sufficiently powerful programming language, the most common languages are C++ or C# for all devices, Flash ActionScript or HTML5 for browsers, and Java or Objective C for mobile devices. These are good options if you are aiming to eventually get hired by an existing game studio, but plenty of independent games are created using Python, Ruby, or JavaScript.

## Part 2. Creating the Game

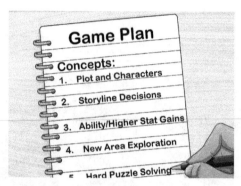

1. Create a plan for the game. Flesh out the concept of the game as much as you can before you begin, including the genre, mood, and type of gameplay. If you start programming before the concept is clear, you'll likely have to tear apart and rewrite a significant amount of work. This will probably happen anyway, but a solid plan will keep these events to a minimum.

- All but the most experimental games have a progress arc, so this is a good place to start the planning. Progress typically happens through one or more of the following: discovering more about the plot and characters, making decisions that affect the storyline, gaining new abilities or higher stats, exploring new areas, or solving harder and harder puzzles.

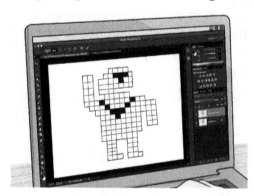

2. Gather your art assets. Collect or create all the textures, sprites, sounds, and models you will need for your game. There are quite a few collections of free game assets, so do some searching. If you are making a 2D game and don't have an artist to help out, you could create your own pixel art.

3. Script your game. The script tells the engine what to do and when to do it. If you used an open

source engine, chances are that it already has a scripting language, and probably tutorials that will teach you how to use it. If you build your own engine then you will have to create your own scripting language. Either way, you'll need these major components at minimum:

- A constantly running game loop that checks for user input, processes the result, processes other events, calculates what needs to be displayed, and sends this to the graphics card. This should run at least 30 times per second.

- "Active listener" scripts that check for events and respond when they occur. For example, one script can watch for a player interacting with a door, then run the "open" animation and make the doorway non-collidable. Another script can watch for a weapon hitbox contacting the door, and run the "blow apart" animation instead.

4. Create individual levels. Level design — which may involve a literal "level 1," an area the player can explore, or the next round of a fighting game — will test some skills unrelated to programming. Start with a simple level showcasing typical gameplay, following this basic guideline for genres that involve traveling through environments:

- Create the basic outline of the area.

- Decide on the basic path the player will most often take through the area. Add challenges and benefits (items) along this path. Space them close together for adrenaline and excitement, or farther apart for a more relaxed atmosphere.

- Start adding graphical elements. Place light sources along the main path to encourage players to follow it, and keep the side paths or less important areas dim.

- Match the gameplay, style, and setting. For example, a suspenseful horror game thrives on stretches of empty exploration punctuated by surprise attacks. A never-ending barrage of enemies overwhelms the player with adrenaline instead, while combat that requires careful tactical planning can distract the player from the emotional atmosphere.

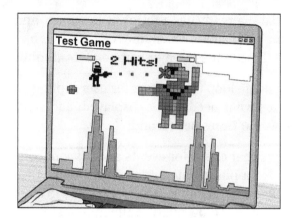

5. Test your game. Now you get to see what all your hard work has turned into. Test each level while you are polishing it, and many times after it is "finished." Make a conscious attempt to play the game in ways you didn't intend, such as playing through more difficult areas first. Better yet, find playtesters to get fresh eyes on the game, and ask for as much feedback as possible.

- Watch someone play without giving them advice, unless it's basic tutorial information that hasn't been added to the game yet. Frustrating mistakes and points where the player gets "stuck" are signs that you need to include more guidance.

- Once the game (or at least a level) is fairly complete, try to find strangers or acquaintances to help playtest. Friends tend to be more optimistic, which is great for providing encouragement but not as helpful for predicting how players will react.

6. Take the next step. If you finish the project, you may want to release it for free or put it up for sale, but make sure you read the terms and conditions for any game engines or software you used. Whether or not you complete the game as you envisioned it, you may want to "cannibalize" some assets and ideas for a different or more ambitious project, or take the lessons you learned and start all over again.

## How to Design a Video Game Level

A Little Guidance to make a good level for your video games/storyline crossover.

## Steps

1. A level plays an important part in the game. But first, lets get to the storyline.

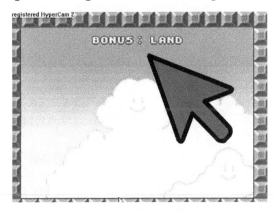

2. Give a reason for why the player is on that specific level they are currently on,or also is known as a Storyline. Story lines are the most important thing in a video game.With out the story line, the player will start to be confused on why they are on the current level. Take Kingdom Hearts for example. Sora is the wielder of the Keyblade, goes on a journey, going to other worlds finding and doing what he needs to do.

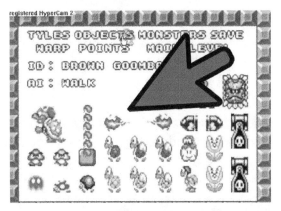

3. Get specific. The storyline is about the keyblade wielder,going around to other worlds and do what has to be done. But Exactly why? why does Sora need to go to these other worlds? without get specific, the player will continue to wonder why.

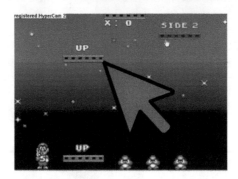

4. Now think of level theme, and think of the storyline first before you just go ahead and put down the level.Every level MUST have a theme.Is it a jungle? A mountain range? Or a savanna?Make a water theme level closer to the beginning so the player can get used to the swimming controls,just in case if there's another water themed level.

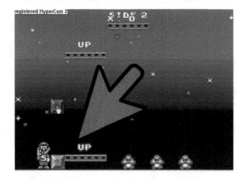

5. Start making levels. with the storyline and level themes fixed up, it's time for the levels.The level plays the 2nd most important role in the game. without levels, the game is just never ending, like World of Warcraft, there is no levels to play on.

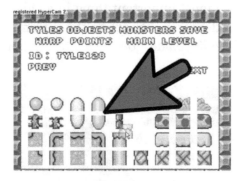

6. Put the finishing touches. now you can add the animation of characters, put the enemies into role, and anything else you might want to add into your game. Good Luck.

## How to make a Video Game Level

When making a video game a very important step is the levels. It's hard to decide what to make some levels but with this guide it can become a lot easier.

## Steps

1. First off decide upon what kind of game you're making. If it's a non-linear, explore-everything game like Banjo-Kazooie or Legend of Zelda then every level should be a different theme and be very spread out. If it's a linear war game like Halo or Call of Duty make it a campaign and each level is in a predesignated order.

- If it's the latter it's rather easy to think up of levels so long as you have a plot.

- If it's the former than it's a lot trickier since you have to think up of various themes to run through with 5-10 levels.

2. Always make each level center around a single theme. For example if its covered in

cemeteries and graveyard it's horror-themed and if it's taking place in a Himalaya-like place it's ice-themed.

- One of most frequently-used (and clever) themes is horror. Of course when it comes to horror make it Halloween-ish horror (the holiday) not Hellraiser-ish horror.

- An absolute must for every non-linear game is a water-themed level. Try to introduce it early on such as Level 4 or Level 5 which is when the game should begin turning difficult. The point is to get the player more oriented to swimming (no matter how badly the controls handle) for later in the game.

3. When it comes to music think what would fit best. The Banjo-Kazooie series is ground-breaking in this regard since every level's music sounds exactly as it should. The level that consists of a

polluted harbor is quirky and low-pitched whilst the level that consists of the 4 seasons each has a different music for each season: a cheery, chirpy song for spring, a slow violin tune for summer, an upbeat horn tune for fall and a harp-like tune with tambourines for winter.

4. If you wish to have a boss have the boss fit with the theme of said level. If the level is themed to the Amazon rainforest have a tapir or sloth be the boss. Make sure that under any conditions you don't interchange it (e.g. in a water-themed level you have a desert lizard boss).

5. How difficult it is should depend on how early and/or later in the game it is.

6. If possible try to think up of a theme that has never been done before. Once more the Banjo-Kazooie series is a good example of this. For example beforehand no one had ever tried to make levels like a cargo-loading polluted harbor, the Mesozoic Era, or a forest in the four seasons of the year. Try to think outside the box.

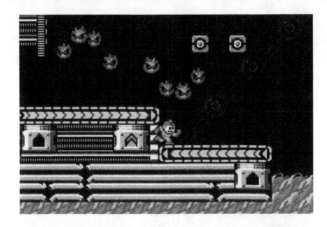

7. The kind of challenges should once again depend on the level's theme. If the level is wind-themed perhaps you need to get something out of a cloud without being set afire away by a strong wind.

## How to make a Video Game Side Quest

Side quests are short optional missions from open world games that might have many different objectives and rewards. They are even more present in role playing games and their finality is to leave the player with things to do as they can be fun and numerous. Here's how to make a side quest.

### Steps

1. Think of the plot, the characters, and what are the tasks for the player. Your side quest will have to be about something, so think what will be the side quest plot and objectives.

- The Plot: Should be a small story with a conflict, as the player will be there as a key to solve it.

- The Objectives: They have to be related to the plot and they can be really different according to it, for example, deliver a message to someone, give something to the X character, go to an X location, or between many other options.

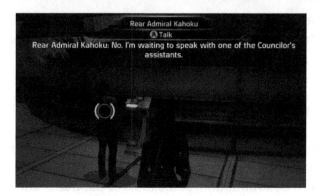

2. Decide how the side quest will start. The start of the side quest will be how the player will be introduced to that small plot. The most common way to do that is to make the player talk to an NPC, but it can be the opposite as the NPC can go and talk to the player when the player reaches a specific place. There are also a few other ways but they are very rare, like making the player find something that makes him curious and drives him to investigate about it.

3. Think of the body of the side quest. Now it's time for the objectives. As mentioned earlier in the first step, one objective can be totally different than another, and is up to you what they will be. Your side quest can have any number of objectives, since a simple one of donating some money to someone - and he only needs that - to one with multiple objectives, like finding out what some evil guy is about to and you would have to check his house first, then talk to him, or whatever.

4. Think of the side quest ending and reward. Last but not least, when the player completes his part on the story, the side quest should have an end and, depending on the side quest and the game, the player should be rewarded. Most of times, a great side quest ending is better than a reward,

since the player should have fun completing the objectives and following the story already. But that doesn't mean that creative rewards like the Wabbajack in Skyrim are really welcome.

## How to make Video Game Music

So, you want to make your own video game music? That's great, because you can get exactly the kind of moods, genres, sound effects, and voice-overs you need. But how does one make music for video games? Well, with determination, some tools of the trade, and a good ear, this topic can provide some of the basics.

### Steps

1. Decide what kind of music you'd like your game to feature. Do you want hardcore metal? Or do you want something a little more soft and classical? You could even use both, if you want. There are absolutely no boundaries to creativity.

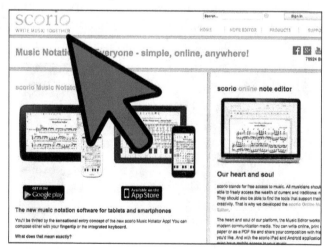

2. Learn how to read and write music. You can do this with either tabs or a music range. Start with a range, since it is the classic way to compose music. Learn all the notes and symbols, and although this may be a long task, it's really worth it.

3. Get the necessary tools If you need any specific instruments or tools, go get them. Look in the Things You'll Need section for sound programs and software.

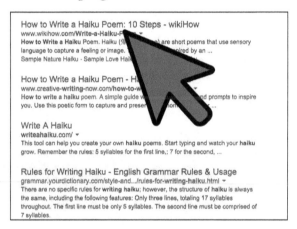

4. Compose. If you need lyrics, write them with a certain rhythm in the syllables. Go see a How to Write a Haiku or Alexandrian Poem entry for help with this. You will also need to know music theory to understand suitable chord progressions, as composing music requires a musical ear; you can't just put any notes together for a work to sound good. Remember the mood and atmosphere you want to create.

5. Record/create. Recording requires many takes, but this is normal. Depending on what kind of tools you are using, this could mean a makeshift recording studio or just a computer. Of course,

if you are using real instruments, you will need to record it. Different music software will let you create music as well as edit it, so choose the one that's right for you.

6. Create sound effects. It will take tons of work, but this step is worth it. This is a really fun part in making the music, because it is so different from the rest of the recording. If you want realistic sound effects, there's no other way around it: you'll have to get out and do exactly what you are creating the sound effect for. Clang utensils or pots for a sword clash, throw heavy rocks down a rocky hill for a destructive sound. There are also sites where you can download sound effects, which are quite useful if you can't get the exact kind of sound you want.

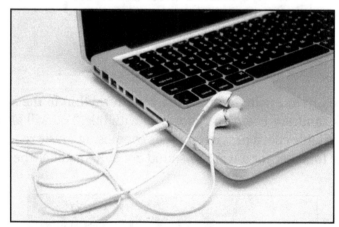

7. Add voice-overs. Again, this will require a lot of starting over and redoing. This part is quite simple: all you need is recording software, a good microphone and a filter (to eliminate spitting sounds and some interference), and a group of people that will bring your characters to life. This part can or cannot be essential, but it may be useful. First and foremost, write your script. Look for a How to Write Theatre Scripts guide for this one. The voice actors usually have their scripts right in front of them, so don't worry on remembering it right (although you certainly will after all the tries). Do not forget to project the cut scene so that the actors can match the lip movement, if necessary. Recording as a group instead of each voice individually makes the exchange of words more natural, though the other actors will have to keep quiet when one is speaking.

8. Edit, compile it, and add it to the game. You can do this using recording software. Make sure you're really familiar with your software; read manuals and/or watch how-to videos. Then you'll be all done and ready to test your game.

## How to make a Game Engine

A game engine is used to simplify the programming process by reusing code from old games. Since most games are similar programming wise (they all have audio, collision detection, etc.), you can reuse a good portion of the code instead of starting from scratch each time.

There are a wide variety of game engines out there. Some geared towards artists with little to no programming required. Some are entirely comprised of GUI's that can make programming easier. And some are made for programmers only.

The information provided here is useful for people interested in making that last kind of engine, for programmers exclusively. Even if you don't know any programming or programming languages, but you are interested in programming or game management, then read on.

### Part 1. Learn to Program

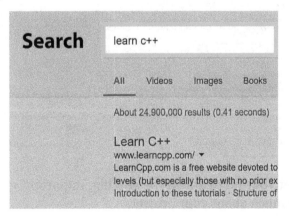

1. Choose your Language. There are a variety of languages from which programs are made. The language you choose doesn't matter too much, but the most important thing is that you start somewhere.

- There are many programming languages to choose from, but most go with C++ or Java and they are also the most useful in Game Development.

- Once you learn one language, it's much easier to learn another.

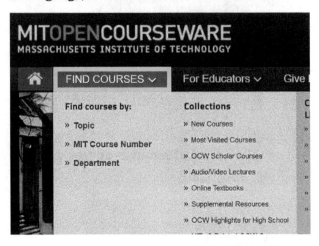

2. Find a course. The most effective way (in my opinion) to learn programming/computer science is to take a class. Whether this is a class at your school, or outside of school shouldn't matter.

- No matter who you are, you can find a programming class that suits you.

- MIT OpenCourseWare has a variety of free classes.

- If you look around on Google, you'll find a number of other sites that also have free lectures and classes available.

- You could also have a friend teach you a language, sharing is caring.

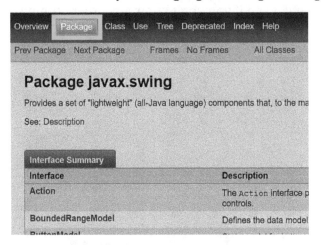

3. Practice. You don't want your first game to be you big, important game. You want a chance to screw up and not care too much about your project.

- Try to make a simple game.

- If you learned Java, check out the Swing package.

- Don't worry too much about this project(s), they should only take up a few weeks of your time.

- Learn from your mistakes.

## Part 2. Start your Game (Engine)

1. Think of a Game Idea. Try to challenge yourself. That way if you don't achieve all you set out to, you'll still (probably) have a pretty good game left over.

- Think for a while, don't feel pressured to do this in one sitting.

- Sit on your idea for a while so you know it is good.

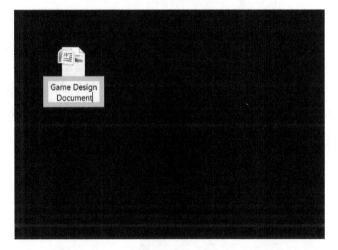

2. Formalize your Idea. Technical communications is important in any kind of engineering, including software engineering. You don't want to tell someone that you're making an apple and they go and make you audio for a pear.

- Write up a "Game Design Document". These are used in professional game development, but more importantly, they easily communicate your idea(s) to others. There are many free templates available online.

3. Recruit Help. You don't have to go at this alone. It's also more fun and exciting in a group.

- You can't make a custom game engine and manage the project without help.

- Ask your Friends first before going to strangers or advertising for help, you'd be surprised who would love to get into the game industry.

**Part 3. Get to Work**

1. Research. Look into what you're going to do before you do it. Even when you make an engine from scratch, there are still a number of tools that you could make your engine out of.

- Look into "OpenGL" if you learned C and "JOGL" if you learned Java.

- Maybe buy a textbook on OpenGL, "Redbook" is the most famous one, but it is online for free.

2. Draw Something. Render a primitive or 2D object to get started.

- Make a 2D triangle, or a cube.

- Look into "Display Lists" so you can draw many primitive objects.

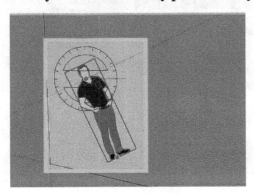

3. Make Perspective. There aren't many games where you can't change where you're looking.

- Make the perspective of your game (First person perspective, top-down, etc.)

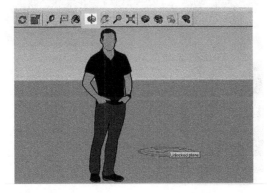

4. Move Around. One step at a time. Except not actually because stepping is actually kind of complicated.

- Either move everything around the camera or move the camera view port, but they are the same to the processor.

- Be able to move in all angles, not just along the axis.

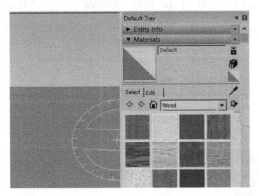

5. Add Textures (Images). That default color will get old after a while, and not many games are used with only solid colors.

- Splice them into your display list(s).

6. Add Audio. This makes your game much more interesting and realistic.

- Perhaps footsteps for when you walk.

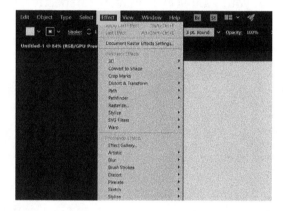

7. Add Lighting. This also adds to the realism.

- Learn the different kinds of lighting.

- Use a sphere instead of a cube to make sure the lighting is working.

- You could put a primitive object where the light should be coming from to debug. Just make sure the light can get out of the box/sphere you put it into.

```
function collisionDetection() {
    for(c=0; c<brickColumnCount; c++) {
        for(r=0; r<brickRowCount; r++) {
            var b = bricks[c][r];
            // calculations
        }
    }
}
```

8. Add Collision Detection. The biggest thing people notice when you show them an incomplete game engine is the lack of proper collision detection.

- Make it impossible to walk through the cube.

- Make it possible to move (in other directions) when you are colliding with the cube.

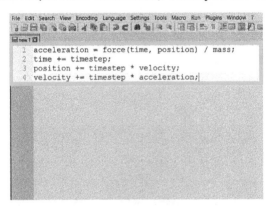

9. Add Gravity. Most games have falling things somewhere.

- Make a floor, and jump around on it.

## Part 4. Finish Business

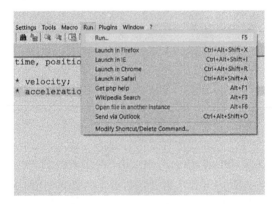

1. Finish Your Game. Don't forget to market it. You may want to enlist a marketer (friend) to help you. Assume your game is going to be a hit so that way you can work towards that.

- Have Fun.

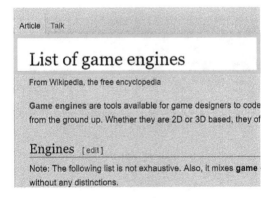

2. Manage Other Games. Don't be coy, tell other developers that you made a game engine. You

don't have to be the only one to develop with your engine. When you let other people use it, you have the right to some of their royalties, but also you get constructive feedback and perhaps improvements to your engine.

- Game Engines are valuable and impressive.

- Did you notice how much those other engines are charging indie developers? (You could be that engine.)

- Use your engine to get wannabe game developers into the industry.

3. Good Luck. Start your journey into the booming game industry.

- Now you can laugh at your friends who said "Unity was easier".

## How to Code a Video Game

Creating a video game is a huge undertaking, but the end result may be the most exciting coding project you've ever completed. You'll learn most from the tools that fit your level of programming knowledge, so don't assume that starting from scratch is the best option. Select a programming language, an Integrated Development Environment, and/or game-making software that you can start to figure out within fifteen minutes of opening it or reading the tutorial.

### Part 1. Choosing an Engine

1. Learn about game engines. Most video games are made using a specialized engine that allows

you to "script" events, characters, and so forth without having to code each one from scratch. Creating a full game engine from scratch can take years, so most independent developers use an existing engine. You'll only need to follow one of the following steps, depending on how comfortable you are with programming and how much time you want to spend on the little details.

2. Consider simple game-making software. These tools require very little programming knowledge, so they may not be for you if you're interested in the coding aspects of game-making. On the other hand, a simple dive-right-in approach could teach you a lot about your game, and let you tweak the higher-level concept before you move on to a larger prototype. Here are several free options:

- For mobile games, try MIT App Inventor or Game Salad.

- For browser games, try Scratch, or the more serious version Snap. intended as an introductory programming tool.

- For adventure games, use Visionaire.

- If you want a drag-and-drop program with the option to delve into coding as well, try the free version of GameMaker.

3. Try more professional development interfaces. This is a great option for getting your hands dirty, getting game-coding experience without having to start completely from scratch. Many professional independent game developers start at this level. While there are many engines and

Integrated Development Environments (IDEs) available, the following are free and relatively easy to learn:

- For mobile games: ProjectAnarchy.

- For 3D games on any platform: Unity.

- For more advanced coders: LWJGL (based in Java), SFML (based in C++).

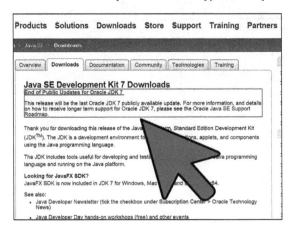

4. Choose a tool for building your own engine. If you already have some programming knowledge and are dead set on building your own engine, here are a few places to get started. If this is your first attempt, you'll likely need tutorials

- ActionScript will let you make a Flash-based engine. This is a good place to start for intermediate programmers.

- Java is relatively simple to learn. You'll need a Java Development Kit (JDK), plus Eclipse or another Integrated Development Environment (IDE) for Java. If you're not sure how to get started.

- If you already know a programming language (especially a C language or Python), look for an IDE for that language. It should include a compiler and the ability to easily work on graphics, audio, and other code in the same project.

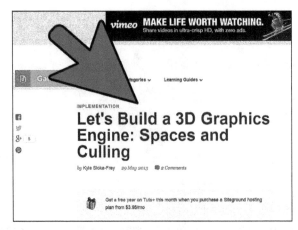

5. Build your own engine. If you are up to the challenge and chose one of the advanced tools in the

previous step, you will most likely need to find a tutorial, a help forum, or an experienced game developer for advice specific to your language. If you're not sure where to start or what to ask about, here are a few basic components you'll need to build early on:

- A client-side server, which interprets user input and processes the result. Make the input system responding correctly before you put serious work into graphics and gameplay. (Try researching "action listeners" if you're stuck.)

- AI for other characters, so they react to the user's actions. For a simpler project, just have the characters move and act in a set path.

- Ability to render graphics (put together and send instructions to the graphics card).

- A game loop that runs constantly while the game is executed. This should take user input, process it, process other game logic (such as enemy movement, background animation, and triggered events), calculate what needs to be drawn (displayed on screen), and send the information to the graphics card. Run this at least 30 times per second (30 fps) if your system can handle it.

## Part 2. Designing the Game

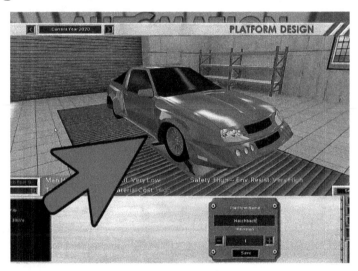

1. Nail down your concept first. Spend a good amount of time nailing down what your game *is* before you touch a line of code. What genre is it? Is it 2D or 3D? Does the player progress in the game by solving puzzles, following/creating the story, fighting enemies, and/or exploring? The more questions you answer and the more detail you give your ideas, the more time you'll save in the long run. If you decide to make a major change after you've already started coding, the change can take many times longer to implement.

- Pare this down to something way, way simpler than your original idea. A small prototype that explores how your game works and gives a couple levels to play is an excellent start. Once it's finished, you can use it as a foundation to expand into a full game, or incorporate what you learned into a new project.

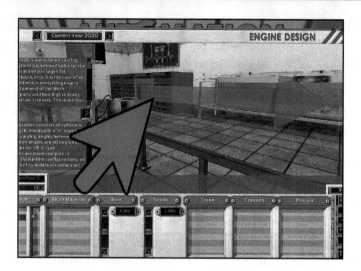

2. Work on the steps below in any order. At this point, there are weeks or months of hard but rewarding work ahead of you. While a team of people will generally divide up the tasks below and work on them simultaneously, an individual will have to decide which task is easiest to start with or most important at each stage. Read through all the steps below and start on the task that appeals to you most.

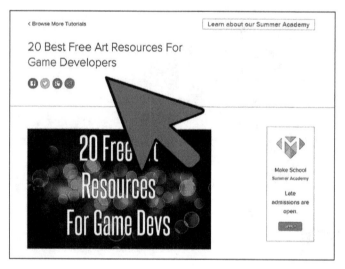

3. Gather or create art assets. Unless you're making at text-base game, you'll need 2D images, and possibly 3D models and textures (patterns you apply to the models). Music and sound effects you can delay until a bit later in the process, but they are highly recommended if you plan to publish your game. Simple icons, user interface, and fonts are lowest-priority when your game is young, but a little effort here can greatly improve the player experience.

- There are many places to find free or cheap art assets online.

- Hiring an artist will make a big difference. If you can't afford to, gather the assets yourself and show the result to artistic friends or post it to game development or art forums online for advice.

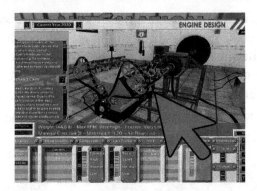

4. Work on story or progress arc design. Much of this will be written as planning documents outside the game code itself, although a story-based game may need to include branching dialogue trees. Even a game without a traditional story should have a sense of progression that you need to plan around. A platformer could involve a series of movement and weapon upgrades, while a puzzle game might add more features as it ramps up the complexity and difficulty of the puzzles.

5. Work on level design. Start with a small, simple level or area. Focus on constructing the path the player takes through the level, then add side paths (optional), more detailed graphics, and tweak the difficulty (such as by adjusting platform heights or moving enemies around).

   • Use light sources and item drops to guide the player to the next spot in the area. Use shadows to discourage players from entering dead-ends or awkward paths, and use enemies for both purposes (depending on how the game teaches you to bypass enemies). A well-designed area makes the player feel like he is making his own decisions or exploring, but guides him along the most straightforward route using subtle clues.

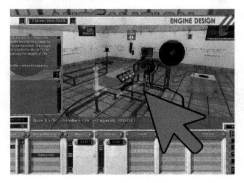

6. Tweak and optimize the graphics. This is not necessary if you are using simple game-making

software. If you are willing to delve into the deeper end of graphics systems, you can start by creating shaders and particle effects, or going through the graphics code and removing tasks that are unnecessary for your game. Because graphics are almost always the choke point that determines processing speed, even a 2D game usually goes through significant optimization tweaks and rewrites in order to minimize the burden on the graphics card and processor.

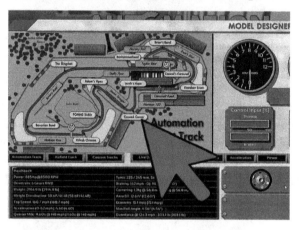

7. Get feedback from playtesters. Once you have a simple level or a prototype of gameplay, have your friends play the game and offer feedback. Find out what people think is fun, and what frustrates them. Later on in the process, when the game is more polished, feedback from strangers or acquaintances can be an excellent source of honest advice, as they are less invested in your success or encouraging you.

- Players are not trained to offer feedback from a developer's perspective. If players dislike an aspect of the game, there's usually something about it that could be improved but the specific suggestions the players make are often not useful. Ask them very specific questions to discover the exact features that bother them.

## How to Design a Multiplayer Level for an Action Game

**Steps**

1. Balance is key. For team games, you don't want one side to overpower the other.

2. Perfect symmetry is bad. You want to have differences between the two sides. For example, if you give one side a big wall of cover, give the other side a hill. This is balanced but not symmetrical.

3. Make sure you can also do free-for-all games, too, but also team games.

4. Don't put all the weapons or powerups in one spot; spread them out.

5. Don't make any one spot better than the other. If you have a spot with a powerful turret, make sure it can be shot at, because you don't want there to be a single, overpowering player.

# Creating Different Types of Video Games

**3**

Video games can be classified into three important categories- casual games, serious games and educational games. This chapter examines the different types of video games such as flash games, educational games, virtual games, CMD adventure, etc. and the ways to create them.

## How to Create an Enjoyable Educational Video Game

With video games becoming more prevalent in the past years, many educational institutions have begun implementing them as a means of teaching. Games provide instant feedback to their users in a way that most other teaching methods can't. Many people, from game designers to teachers may be interested in creating their own educational games. While creating a game of any type isn't going to happen overnight, it is definitely a feasible task for anyone willing to invest some time in the process.

### Part 1. Analyzing

1. Determine what you are trying to teach. The topic of an educational game could be anything from how to cook a simple meal to advanced particle physics. The first thing you need to do is determine what sort of subject matter you want your game to illustrate. Whatever you decide here will become the basis for the game you create.

2. Determine the depth of your knowledge on your chosen subject. It is very difficult to teach

something that you're not deeply familiar with. Take time to ask yourself, "would I be able to teach this subject to my target audience in a classroom?" While you don't need ultimate knowledge on every field related to your game's topic, you should posses a very firm grasp on the concepts you're trying to teach. Take some time to research your topic here if necessary.

3. Determine the depth of your knowledge on game design. It's alright if you've never designed a game before. There are many in depth tutorials on most aspects of video game design, programming, and asset creation available on YouTube. Even though you don't need a great deal of experience to make a game, creating a good game will require some understanding of the design process and video games themselves.

4. Understand the difference between an educational game and a game which happens to be educational. While there is no set definition of a good video game, no one with any experience playing games will hesitate to point out a bad one. Educational games of the 90's focused primarily on teaching a topic, adding in gameplay like functions as an afterthought. No matter how technically accurate and educational your game is, it won't do any good if it doesn't hold the player's attention long enough to get your topics across. A good educational game should focus on gameplay and build education into the system.

5. Research similar games and concepts. Are there any existing games about your subject? What other educational materials on the subject exist? Being mindful of prior art is important because it allows you to draw inspiration without knowingly (or not) encroaching on any copyright.

## Part 2. Designing

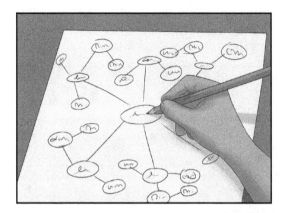

1. Brainstorm. Everyone brainstorms in a different way. Some people do it alone with index cards or a notepad while others prefer to brainstorm in a group with a white board or collaboration software. The point of this step is to generate more than enough ideas related to your topic to give you something to go with. Don't worry if some of your ideas seem to be well off track, because you will narrow them down later.

2. Define the scope of your topic. The topic you want to teach should be broad enough that players without prior knowledge will still be able to benefit, but not so broad that the educational bits will get lost in the openness of the game. Try to find a balance between an all encompassing game and one which dwells over specific details of a specific topic.

3. Choose a genre/gameplay style. This choice should be based on what you're trying to teach. For

example, a real time strategy game or first person shooter would be poorly suited to teach physics. Likewise, a side-scrolling platformer would have a difficult time conveying the details of algebra. Note: There are exceptions to this, such as Valve Software's Portal game can be implemented to teach physics lessons.

4. Understand your audience. Will your target audience be a room full of third graders or adults trying to further education? Understanding the target audience at an early stage will help you tailor the game to a level that will entertain them. Younger audiences will need likely to be helped throughout their play through of your game, while older audiences may feel insulted if you do the same thing. Try to limit your audience to as few groups as possible.

5. Drop ideas that don't fit or feel right. No matter how great an idea is, if it doesn't fit with the theme of your game, valuable resources (such as time, energy, and money) will be wasted on it. Don't feel obligated to incorporate every good idea that comes up into your game. You will have other opportunities to use those ideas in later projects. There is an old adage in film, "If you can cut a scene and have the movie still make sense, cut it."

# Part 3. Implementing

1. Prepare your chosen software. Now that the analysis and design stages are completed, it is time to get ready for action. Make sure that you have access to a reliable (and internet connected) computer with all of the software that you will need. The software will vary greatly from person to person depending on the scope of your project and what you're comfortable with.

2. Get others onboard. Unless you're tackling this project by yourself (which will be difficult, although not impossible), feel free to enlist the help of other people. Depending on where you're coming from or the scope of your project, these people could be friends or family members with coding or art skills, or paid professionals who know exactly what they're doing. There is no shame working on this by yourself, just understand the resources that you have available and don't overstretch the scope of your abilities. Utilize the resources that others have.

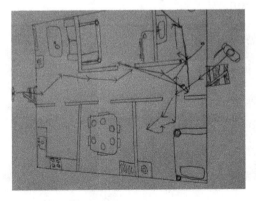

3. Create a Paper Prototype. This step is optional and often overlooked, but can be used to diagnose any potential problems and generate better ideas before any coding takes place. Think of every

mechanic and system in your game, then make a paper version of it. This will let you see how you want key pieces of your game to interact and lets you make any adjustments to your idea before ever writing any code.

4. Program your back end. The details of this will vary greatly depending on the engine and IDE (integrated development environment) you're using, but the advice is the same. Starting with a solid back end will greatly reduce the number of problems you encounter later in your project. Take your time to make sure all of your systems are working together correctly before implementing anything else.

5. Program your user interaction and/or character. Not all types of games place the player in control of a character. If you have chosen a genre that allows the player to directly manipulate their environment, program that now. If you have a playable character, this is a good time to work on the controls and basic animation.

6. Design your User Interface (UI). Even though this is generally the last step in implementing a game, special attention should be paid to the user interface. This is how the player will spend most

of their time interacting with your game and if it isn't intuitive to the player, they won't enjoy the game as much as you would like.

## Part 4. Testing

1. Find people willing to play test your game. Friends and family may work for small projects, but if you don't make it clear that you need honest feedback on your game they may tell you what you want to hear to protect your feelings. Many colleges and universities have game clubs which will play test your game for free. Larger projects may require professional play testers.

2. Determine if the player learned what you intended. Don't directly ask them this question, but ask them questions about the subject matter. It should be clear by their answers whether your topic material got through to them. You may want to prepare some quiz-like questions to evaluate whether the topic was entirely understood.

3. Determine if the player enjoyed the game. You can directly ask them this question, but most people won't be able to give a direct reason. Watching the way they play and monitoring their

expression will give you a much more accurate idea. The point of creating an enjoyable educational game is that the player enjoys it, so this is the most important step in the testing phase.

4. Determine if the player had any difficulty playing the game. Don't guide them through the game if they get stuck on a puzzle or with part of your UI or control scheme. Mark these down as problem areas which need to be fixed. Ask for feedback while they're playing and what they're thinking/attempting to do.

5. Repeat the previous main steps (as needed) until you are satisfied. Now that you have completed the first iteration of your game, determine whether or not you are satisfied. Did the players enjoy the game you created? Did they learn anything from it? If so, you've created an enjoyable educational game. If not, you can go back to part 1 and begin the process again with all of the information you've gathered from testing. Through this iterative process, your game will become better and many of the problems will be worked out.

## How to make a Flash Game

Flash is a popular format for browser-based video games seen on sites such as Newgrounds and Kongregate. While the Flash format is slowly becoming less-utilized in the face of growing mobile apps, many quality games are still being made with it. Flash uses ActionScript, an easy-to-learn language that gives you control over the objects on your screen.

### Part 1. Starting the Process

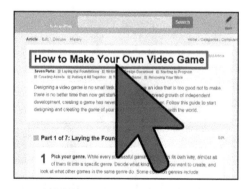

1. Design your game. Before you start coding, it will help to have a rough idea of what you want

your game to do. Flash is best suited for simple games, so focus on creating a game that has only a few mechanics for the player to worry about. Try to have a basic genre and some mechanics in mind before you start prototyping. Common Flash games include:

- Endless runners: These games automatically move the character, and the player is responsible for jumping over obstacles or otherwise interacting with the game. The player typically only has one or two options when it comes to controls.

- Brawlers: These are typically sidescrolling and task the player with defeating enemies to progress. The player character often has several moves that they can perform to defeat enemies.

- Puzzles: These games ask the player to solve puzzles to beat each level. These can range from Match-3 style such as Bejeweled to more complex puzzle solving typically found in Adventure games.

- RPGs: These games focus on character development and progression, and have the player moving through multiple environments with a variety of enemy types. Combat mechanics vary wildly from RPG to RPG, but many are turn-based. RPGs can be significantly more difficult to code than a simple action game.

2. Learn what Flash excels at. Flash is best-suited for 2D games. It is possible to create 3D games in Flash, but it is very advanced and requires significant knowledge of the language. Almost every successful Flash game has been 2D.

- Flash games are also best suited for quick sessions. This is because most Flash game players play when they have a little free time, such as on breaks, meaning gaming sessions are typically 15 minutes or less.

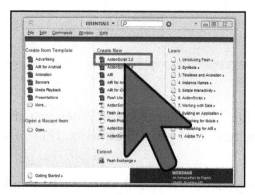

3. Familiarize yourself with the ActionScript3 (AS3) language. Flash games are programmed in

AS3, and you will need to have some basic understanding of how it works in order to successfully create a game. You can create a simple game with a rudimentary understanding of how to code in AS3.

- There are several books about ActionScript available on Amazon and other stores, along with a large number of tutorials and examples online.

4. Download Flash Professional. This program costs money, but is the best way to create Flash programs quickly. There are other options available, including open-source options, but they often lack compatibility or take longer to accomplish the same tasks.

- Flash Professional is the only program you will need to start creating games.

**Part 2. Writing a Basic Game**

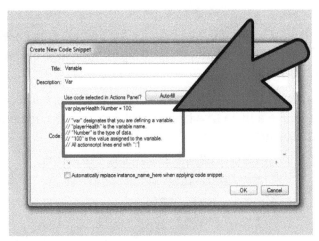

1. Understand the basic building blocks of AS3 code. When you are creating a basic game, there are several different code structures that you will be using. There are three main parts of any AS3 code:

- Variables - This is how your data is stored. Data can be numbers, words (strings), objects, and more. Variables are defined by the code var and must be one word.

```
var playerHealth:Number = 100;
```

// "var" designates that you are defining a variable.

// "playerHealth" is the variable name.

// "Number" is the type of data.

// "100" is the value assigned to the variable.

// All actionscript lines end with ";"

- Event Handlers - Event handlers look for specific things to occur, and then tells the rest of the program. This is essential for player input and repeating code. Event handlers typically call upon functions.

```
addEventListener(MouseEvent.CLICK, swingSword);
```

// "addEventListener()" defines the event handler.

// "MouseEvent" is the category of input that is being listened for.

// ".CLICK" is the specific event in the MouseEvent category.

// "swingSword" is the function that is called when the event occurs.

- Function - Sections of code assigned to a keyword that can be called upon later. Functions handle the bulk of your game's programming, and complex games can have hundreds of functions while simpler games may only have a few. They can be in any order since they only work when they are called upon.

```
function swingSword (e:MouseEvent):void;

{

        //Your code goes here

}
```

// "function" is the keyword that appears at the start of every function.

// "swingSword" is the name of the function.

// "e:MouseEvent" is an added parameter, showing that the function

// is called from the event listener.

// ":void" is the value that is returned by the function. If no value

// is returned, use :void.

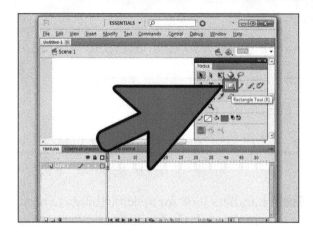

2. Create an object. ActionScript is used to affect objects in Flash. In order to make a game, you will need to create objects that the player will interact with. Depending on the guides you are reading, objects may be referred to as sprites, actors, or movie clips. For this simple game, you will be creating a rectangle.

- Open Flash Professional if you haven't already. Create a new ActionScript 3 project.

- Click the Rectangle drawing tool from the Tools panel. This panel may be in different locations depending on the configuration of Flash Professional. Draw a rectangle in your Scene window.

- Select the rectangle using the Selection tool.

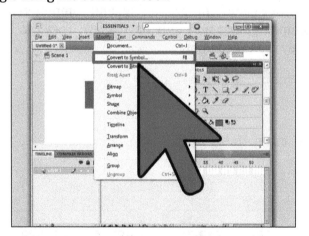

3. Assign properties to the object. With your newly-created rectangle selected, open the Modify menu and select "Convert to Symbol". You can also press F8 as a shortcut. In the "Convert to Symbol" window, give the object an easily recognizable name, such as "enemy".

- Find the Properties window. At the top of the window, there will be a blank text field labeled "Instance name" when you hover over it. Name it the same as you did when you converted it to a symbol ("enemy"). This creates a unique name that can be interacted with through AS3 code.

- Each "instance" is a separate object that can be affected by code. You can copy the already created instance multiple times by clicking the Library tab and dragging the instance onto the scene. Each time you add one, the name will be changed to designate that it's a separate object ("enemy", "enemy1", "enemy2", etc.).

- When you refer to the objects in the code, you simply need to use the instance name, in this case "enemy".

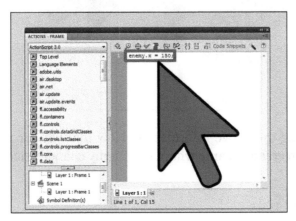

4. Learn how you can change the properties of an instance. Once you have an instance made, you can adjust the properties through AS3. This can let you move the object around the screen, resize it, and so on. You can adjust properties by typing the instance, followed by a period ".", followed by the property, followed by the value:

- `enemy.x = 150;` This affects the position of the enemy object on the X-axis.

- `enemy.y = 150;` This affects the position of the enemy object on the Y-axis. The Y-axis is calculated from the top of the scene.

- `enemy.rotation = 45;` Rotates the enemy object 45° clockwise.

- `enemy.scaleX = 3;` Stretches the width of the enemy object by a factor of 3. A (-) number will flip the object.

- `enemy.scaleY = 0.5;` Squishes the object to half its height.

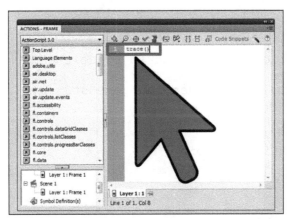

5. Examine the trace() command. This command will return the current values for specific objects, and is useful for determining if everything is running as it should. You may not want to include the

Trace command in your final code, but it is useful for debugging.

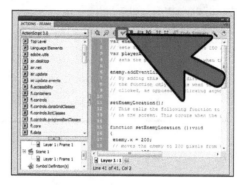

6. Build a basic game using the above information. Now that you have a basic understanding of the core functions, you can create a game where the enemy changes size every time you click on it, until it runs out of health.

```
var enemyHP:Number = 100;

// sets the enemy's HP (health) to 100 at the start.

var playerAttack:Number = 10;

// sets the players attack power when they click.


enemy.addEventListener(MouseEvent.CLICK, attackEnemy);

// By adding this function directly to the enemy object,

// the function only happens when the object itself is

// clicked, as opposed to clicking anywhere on the screen.


setEnemyLocation();

// This calls the following function to place the enemy

// on the screen. This occurs when the game starts.


function setEnemyLocation ():void

{

 enemy.x = 200;

 // moves the enemy to 200 pixels from the left of the screen

 enemy.y = 150;
```

```
    // moves the enemy down 150 pixels from the top of the screen

    enemy.rotation = 45;

    // rotates the enemy 45 degrees clockwise

    trace("enemy's x-value is", enemy.x, "and enemy's y-value is", enemy.y);

    // Displays the current position of the enemy for debugging

}


function attackEnemy (e:MouseEvent):void

// This creates the attack function for when the enemy is clicked

{

  enemyHP = enemyHP - playerAttack;

  // Subtracts the attack value from the HP value,

  // resulting in the new HP value.

  enemy.scaleX = enemyHP / 100;

  // Changes the width based on the new HP value.

  // It is divided by 100 to turn it into a decimal.

  enemy.scaleY = enemyHP / 100;

  // Changes the height based on the new HP value


  trace("The enemy has", enemyHP, "HP left");

  //Output how much HP the enemy has left

}
```

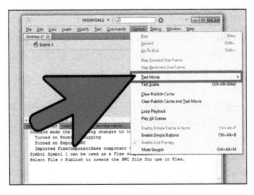

7. Try it out. Once you've created the code, you can test your new game. Click the Control menu and select Test Movie. Your game will begin, and you can click the enemy object to change its size. Your Trace outputs will be displayed in the Output window.

## Part 3. Learning Advanced Techniques

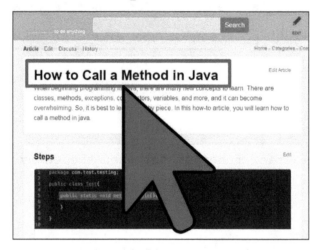

1. Learn how packages work. ActionScript is based off Java, and uses a very similar package system. Packages allow you to store variables, constants, functions, and other information in separate files, and then import these files into your program. These are especially useful if you want to use a package that someone else has developed that will make your game easier to create.

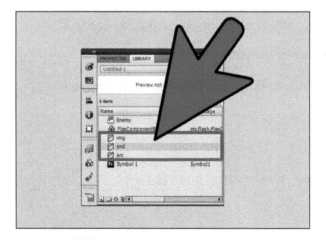

2. Build your project folders. If you're creating a game with multiple images and sound clips, you'll want to create a folder structure for your game. This will allow you to easily store your different elements, as well as store different packages to call on.

- Create a base folder for your project. In the base folder, you should have an "img" folder for all of your art assets, a "snd" folder for all of your sound assets, and a "src" folder for all of your game packages and code.

- Create a "Game" folder in the "src" folder to store your Constants file.

- This particular structure isn't necessary, but is an easy way to organize your work and materials, especially for larger projects. For the simple game explained above, you will not need to create any directories.

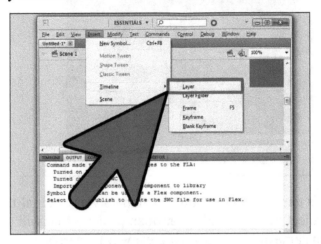

3. Add sound to your game. A game without sound or music will quickly become boring to the player. You can add sound to objects to Flash using the Layers tool.

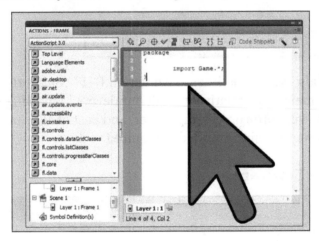

4. Create a Constants file. If your game has a lot of values that will remain the same throughout the game, you can create a Constants file to store all of them in one place so that you can easily call on them. Constants can include values such as gravity, player speed, and any other value that you may need to call on repeatedly.

- If you create a Constants file, it will need to be placed in a folder in your project and then imported as a package. For example, let's say you create a Constants.as file and place it in your Game directory. To import it, you would use the following code:

```
package

{

        import Game.*;

}
```

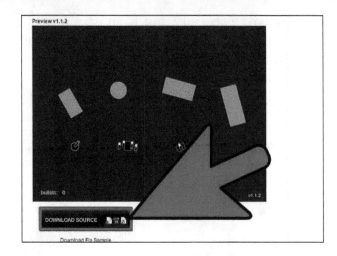

5. Look at other people's games. While many developers won't reveal the code for their games, there are a variety of project tutorials and other open projects that will allow you to see the code and how it interacts with game objects. This is a great way to learn some advanced techniques that can help your game stand out.

## How to make a Text based Game

Text adventure games, also known as interactive fiction ("IF" for short), were the earliest form of computer games and maintain a relatively small but devoted following today. They are usually free to download, take up very little processing power, and best of all, you can create them by your lonesome, without any programming knowledge required.

### Part 1. Choosing the Software

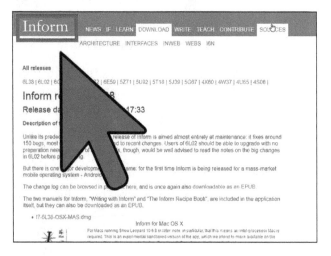

1. Try Inform 7. Inform 7 is a popular and powerful tool for creating text games, more often called interactive fiction. Its programming language is designed to look like simple English sentences, while still allowing full functionality. Inform 7 is free and available for Windows, Mac, and Linux.

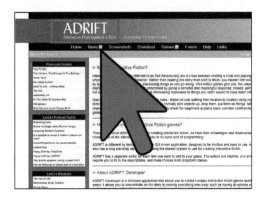

2. Use Adrift for easy game creation on Windows. Adrift is another popular, easy to use interactive fiction language and compiler. Because it relies on a graphical interface instead of coding, it may be the easiest tool for a non-programmer to use. Adrift is free and available for Windows only, although games created with it can be played on any operating system or in a browser.

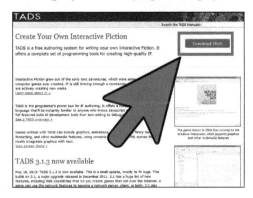

3. Consider TADS 3 if you know some programming. If you'd rather approach text game creation as a coding project, TADS 3 may be the most comprehensive software of this type. It will be especially easy to pick up if you are familiar with C++ and/or Javascript. TADS 3 is free and available for Windows, Mac, and Linux.

- The Windows version (only) of TADS 3 comes with a "Workbench" addition that makes it much more accessible to non-programmers, and more convenient to use in general.

- Programmers may be interested in this in-depth comparison between Inform 7 and TADS 3.

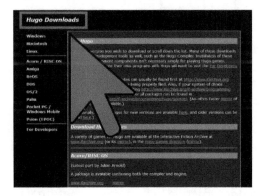

4. Explore other mainstream options. The tools above are by far the most popular, but there are

several others that have strong followings in the interactive fiction community. If none of the tools above interest you or you want to explore more options, try these next:

- Hugo
- ALAN

5. Try a browser-based option. You can jump in and get started without any downloads using one of the following tools:

- Quest (more similar to the IF tools above).
- Twine (easy to use visual editor).
- StoryNexus (the player clicks options instead of guessing what to type; StoryNexus hosts your game online).

## Part 2. Getting Started

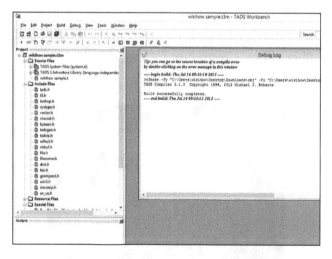

1. Familiarize yourself with text commands. Most text-based games are played by typing in commands. People who have played interactive fiction games before will expect you to include certain commands in your game, such as "examine (object)" and "take (object)".

- The documentation or tutorial for your software should introduce you to these commands, and how to include them in your game.

- Often, a game has additional unique commands, which can be anything from "twirl baton" to "mow lawn." These options should always be made clear to the player, unless you are putting them in as jokes or Easter eggs that are not required to complete the game.

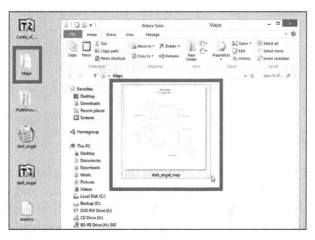

2. Plan out the map and/or player progression. The most common form of interactive fiction involves exploring different locations, usually called "rooms" even if they are outdoors. A good project to start with could include one or two rooms to explore at the start, another couple rooms the player can get to with some simple searching or problem-solving, and a larger puzzle the player needs to solve with some thinking or thorough searching.

- Alternatively, you can make a project that's focused more on the decisions the player makes, instead of the puzzles he solves. This could be an emotional story focused on the player's relationship with other characters, or a plot-based story where the player has many decisions to make, then witnesses the consequences in later scenes. This may still use a geographic map, or it could use "rooms" that are more like scenes, with the player progressing through several vignettes that explore these themes.

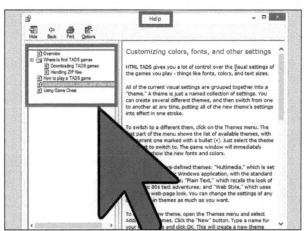

3. Get help with syntax. If your first room doesn't work the way you want it to, or you're just not sure how to achieve what you want with your software, look for a "documentation" or "help" menu,

or a "Read Me" in the same folder as the main tool. If that's not enough, ask your question on a forum at the website where you got the software, or at a general-purpose interactive fiction forum.

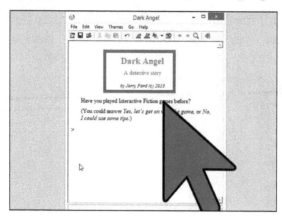

4. Create the introduction and first room. Once you have a basic plan for your game, write a *short* introduction to describe the game, explain any unusual commands, and warn about adult content if any. Next, write the first room description. Try to make the first setting interesting, as many players will walk away if they see an empty apartment. Here's an example of the first thing a player might see when they start up the game (labeled for convenience):

- Introduction: You redeemed your entire collection of pudding coupons for this yacht, and now it's adrift at sea. Typical luck. Better see whether Lucy weathered the storm. You think she was in the engine room when it hit.

- Logistics and content warning: Welcome to *The Frugal Man's Yacht Trip*. Type check coupons to see your current collection. Use the command redeem followed by the name of the coupon to use these mysteriously helpful items. Warning: game depicts mild violence and cannibalism.

- Room description: You are standing in an oak-panelled bunk room. The metal bunk frame fell over during the storm, and the only mattress lies torn and soggy under the liquor cabinet. There is a closed door to the north.

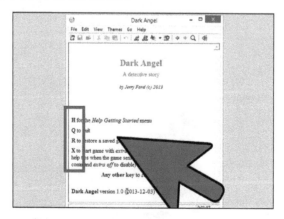

5. Create commands for the first room. Come up with ways for the player to interact with each object you mentioned. At the very least, they should be able to "examine" or "x" each one. Here are a few examples of commands the player can use and the text they see as a result:

- examine mattress – Stuffed with finest quality goose feathers, most of which are now floating around the room. Soggy and smells of booze.

- x me – You are exhausted, and wearing only the ragged pink bathrobe you put on just before the storm hit. The bathrobe has a pocket and a cotton sash.

- open door – The doorknob turns, but won't open. It feels like there's something heavy on the other side.

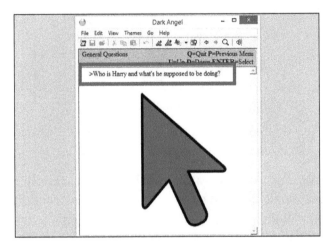

6. Turn the first room into a simple puzzle. A classic beginning requires the player to find a way out of the room. This doesn't have to be a complicated puzzle, just a taste for what your game will be like. It also teaches the player to read carefully and look for hints. For instance, the player might be supposed to do this, after typing the commands above:

- pick up mattress – As soon as you lift it, a reek of tequila assaults your nose. That explains why this mattress is soggy you toss it to the side and wipe your hands on your bathrobe.

- x room – You are standing in an oak-panelled bunk room. The metal bunk frame fell over during the storm, and the only mattress lies torn and soggy in the corner. A liquor cabinet is in the corner. There is a closed door to the north. A broken bottle is on the floor.

- pick up bottle – You pick up the broken bottle of tequila. Waste not, want not.

- x pocket – Your wallet is still there. Phew.

- x wallet – You may have given up the pudding coupons, but you still have your emergency coupon wallet. Right now you have a a crowbar coupon and a whistle coupon.

- redeem crowbar – You hold up the crowbar coupon and clear your throat. The coupon drifts away, and a moment later a hefty crowbar falls into your hand.

- open door with crowbar – You insert the crowbar into the gap of the doorframe and push hard. A growl on the other side startles you. One more attempt should open the door, but you'd better have a weapon ready.

- open door with crowbar – This time there isn't even a weight on the door. It swings open easily, to reveal a large grey wolf staring at you. Better think fast – you can only choose one option.

- hit wolf with bottle – You wallop the wolf right on the nose with the broken bottle. It whimpers and runs off. The way north is now clear.

## Part 3. Polishing and Finishing the Game

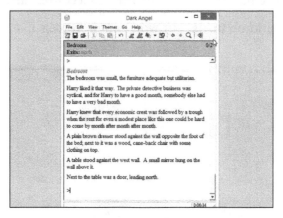

1. Keep verbs and nouns obvious. As the creator, you'll become so familiar with the terms that they seem second nature. Other people only have a few sentences of instruction to work with. Whenever you add a new command or object, especially one that's vital to move forward in the game, make sure you keep it obvious and simple to use.

- Always use valid object names in the room description. For example, if a player walks into the room and sees a description of "a painting," make sure "painting" is the term for that object in your game. If you carelessly use the term "picture" instead, players will have to guess at how to interact with it.

- Allow synonyms for verbs. Take some time to think about how a player might try to use objects. A button should respond to both "push button" and "press button." An enemy should give the option to "attack," "punch," and "hit," plus "use (any item that could be treated as a weapon) on (enemy)."

2. Make your puzzles feel realistic. Don't let your carefully devised puzzle break the reader's immersion in the setting. You might feel terribly clever for creating a puzzle that involves a Viking helmet, a stick of dynamite, and a bee hive, but it's unreasonable to discover these items in a spaceship or a high school classroom. Your setting will feel less cohesive, and the items may as well have a neon sign flashing "use me for a puzzle."

- Giving puzzles more than one solution makes them feel much more realistic, as does allowing a single item to be used in multiple puzzles or in multiple ways.

- Make the puzzles feel relevant. There should be a reason your character needs to solve the puzzle.

- Avoid artificial puzzles such as towers of Hanoi, mazes, and logic puzzles.

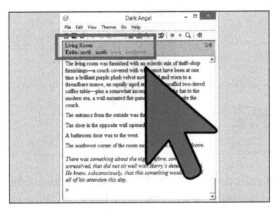

3. Be fair to players. Old-school adventure games are famous for cruel results such as "You pick up the rock, starting an avalanche that buries you. Game over." Nowadays, players want their skill to be rewarded. Besides avoiding arbitrary player deaths, here are a few other design goals to keep in mind:

- Don't make important events hinge on a die roll. For the most part, if a player has figured out what to do, he should succeed 100% of the time.

- Provide hints for difficult puzzles, and don't put in more than two or three red herrings.

- Don't make a puzzle that can't be solved on the first playthrough, such as one that requires knowledge of the next area or a trial-and-error puzzle that kills you if you don't guess correctly.

- It's fine to permanently close off an area partway through the game, but the player should be given fair warning before this happens. If a choice makes the game unwinnable, this should be obvious in advance, and it should end the game instead of letting the player keep trying with no hope of winning.

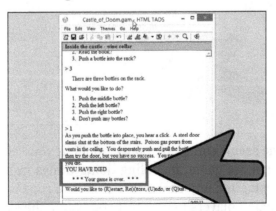

4. Write the endings. Spend some time to make every ending interesting. If the player loses, he should still get to read a sizable chunk of text that describes specifically what happened, and

encourages him to try again. If a player wins, give her a long, triumphant ending, and consider allowing her to spend a couple additional actions savoring the victory in a special end-game room.

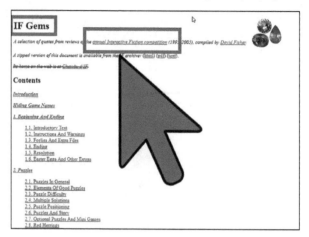

5. Find more advice and inspiration. There are dozens if not hundreds of articles available at Brass Lantern, Interactive Fiction Database, and IFWiki, where you can home in on specialized topics like how to write convincing characters, or how to program objects with complex interactions. Perhaps even more important is the large collection of text-based games at IF Archive, where you can discover what you enjoy firsthand, by playing the games yourself. Here are a few excellent resources to start with:

- The IF Gems collection of quotes

- IF Theory Book

- Craft of Adventure

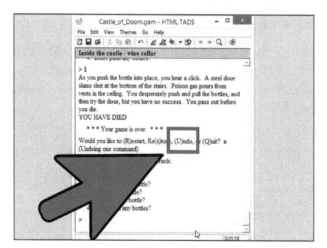

6. Beta test. Once your game seems complete, play through it yourself several times. Try to cover all the possible paths through the game, including doing things in a "weird" sequence that you didn't intend. Once you've corrected any errors that come up, rope in a few friends, family members, or online interactive fiction players to beta test your game the same way. Encourage them to give feedback on what parts were frustrating or not fun, and consider their suggestions for changes or additional options.

- Save often or use the "undo" command, if available, so you can try different paths without starting from the beginning each time.

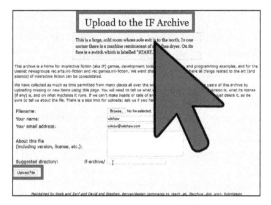

7. Publish. Some text-based game creation software also comes with an online platform where you can upload the game. More commonly, the creator will upload the game to IF Archive, and post a description at IFDB.

- Share links to your game on social media and on interactive fiction forums for more exposure.

- The vast majority of text-based games are offered for free. You can charge money for it, but if this is your first project and you don't have an existing fan base, don't expect many buyers.

## How to Create a Virtual World

Virtual worlds are computer-based simulated environments that you enter with an avatar and sometimes interact with other users inside. Most virtual worlds allow for multiple users and have 2D or 3D graphics. You create, visit or customize fictional environments.

### Part 1. Getting Started in a Virtual World

1. Choose your game platform. There are many sites and video games these days that allow you to create virtual worlds. Some are free, and some cost money. Some are online, and others are available through video gaming consoles.

- Some are role playing games like World of Warcraft. Others are 2D or 3D social networking and virtual worlds like Kaneva and Twinity. Second Life is a popular virtual world with hundreds of thousands of users.

- There are also virtual worlds that are specifically marketed for tweens and teens. Some examples include OurWorld and WoozWorld, which allow you to create an avatar and explore virtual worlds. Online games offer many different virtual world environments, from fantasy worlds to horror and historical environments.

- In some virtual worlds, you get to choose a virtual family. In others, you are able to create your own home and customize it. Some virtual world games have already created worlds that you then get to explore and chat with people inside.

2. Sign up for the online platform. If you're using an online virtual world, like Second Life, you will need to sign up to explore the virtual world. Some of these virtual worlds are free.

- You will be asked to create a username in order to sign in. You will need to login with this name after checking its availability. You may be asked to download the game to your computer before you can use it. Some sites, like Smeet, are browser based and don't require downloads.

- You don't always need to use your real name as your username, although it depends on the game. Many people don't do so because they are trying to explore being a character other than themselves.

- Write down your username so you don't forget it because you will need to use it to log back in. You will likely be asked to create an account using a real email and will perhaps be asked your date of birth and other information.

3. Pick your avatar. An avatar is the character that you will use to represent yourself as you move through the virtual world.

- Many sites allow you to customize your avatar, changing things like hairstyle, eye color, skin color, and gender, as well as clothing. Some sites, like Second Life, allow you to choose vampires as well as people.

- Some people choose avatars that are very similar to themselves. Others decide it would be more interesting to change genders, races, or other attributes.

- It's really up to you (and the site you choose) when it comes to how far you want to make your avatar deviate from yourself. Some avatars are more cartoonish, such as WeeWorld, and others are more sophisticated looking.

## Part 2. Entering the Virtual World

1. Explore the virtual world. Once you have an avatar, it's time to explore the virtual world that you have chosen. Figure out what the virtual world allows you or requires you to do. You will need to figure out the specific controls to move your avatar.

- Learn the rules of the specific game by reading the materials provided before you enter the virtual world. For example, many virtual world games provide frequently asked questions and other instructional materials. In some games, you simply use keys on your computer keyboard to move the avatar and can choose functions that enable your avatar to run, walk, fly or teleport into a new world.

- Spend some time getting to know the virtual world before you change anything in it. Figure out how it works, and go on a journey to see what's in it. Some virtual worlds, like those in WeeWorld, allow you to play games. Some virtual worlds even have a space within the simulated environment where you can go and ask questions about using the virtual world.

- In real life, you would want to scope out and acclimate to your environment before changing anything in it. The same is true in a virtual world. Virtual World.com is an example of an online game that allows you to visit a main street, beach, saloon, and skatepark, among other environments.

2. Interact with other people in the virtual world. Some virtual worlds allow you to interact with other users. Some sites, like Second Life, allow voice as well as text chatting with other users.

- You will see a text chat box pop up with the usernames of other people currently in the world. People have made virtual friends through such worlds. Some people feel more confident in virtual worlds because they are shy in real life. Some virtual worlds also provide maps that show you who else is in the world and where to find them.

- Follow the rules set by the virtual world game for interaction with others. Always be respectful. Just because it's a virtual world doesn't mean you can do anything you want. Sometimes circles of friends will chat with other friends in virtual worlds but they know who each other is outside of the simulated environment.

- Be aware that some people who have taken such interactions off line have found themselves in danger or meeting someone who was not what they imagined. Always be cautious when meeting people online.

3. Figure out how to navigate through the virtual world. Different virtual worlds will have different rules for navigation. You may be able to approach other avatars and interact with them.

- Figure out how you are supposed to move the avatar and where you are allowed to go.

- You may need to perform tasks or pay money to access different levels of the virtual world. You are usually able to travel through different virtual worlds.

- Some virtual worlds will show you a map to help you figure out where you are going inside the virtual world and will offer you multiple world options.

## Part 3. Changing and Experiencing the Virtual World

1. Customize the virtual world. It depends on the game you've chosen, but some virtual worlds will allow you to change aspects of the virtual world.

- You might be able to create and design your own house, pick a job, or even choose the members of a virtual family. Some sites, like Kaneva and SimCity, allow you to create your own virtual worlds and even manage your own cities, whereas other sites allow you to visit and customize preexisting virtual worlds, or both.

- In some virtual worlds, you get to choose a virtual pet or virtual boyfriend or girlfriend. The possibilities are endless. Some virtual worlds allow you to perform some activities for free but make you pay to do extra things, like design a private 3D home to entertain in.

- The power of many virtual worlds is that they allow the user – you. – to both build and to create things. So you are able to unleash the powers of your imagination.

2. Try a virtual reality headset. The most common of these is the Oculus Rift DK2. Some simulation sites allow you to use hardware that creates more of an immerse experience. Other such headsets are in the works or available, such as Vive.

- You put the project viewer over your face like you are wearing goggles. This will allow you to feel like you are actually in the virtual world environment.

- Simply staring at your computer or television screen won't fully immerse you in the virtual world. The Oculus Rift project viewer is designed to make you feel like you are actually inside the virtual world.

- Not all virtual world sites allow or work with such viewers. Second Life is one that does. Viewers are being developed that will mimic your real facial expressions and place them on your avatar.

3. Be aware of the impact of virtual reality. There's a lot of research into virtual worlds that shows they can have both positive and negative effects on people's lives.

- Some researchers believe that spending too much time in virtual worlds can lead to isolation in real life for some people.

- At the same time, some people replace their unhappy realities with a happier virtual world they are more able to control.

- Some people have become addicted to virtual worlds to the degree that it has caused them to neglect their real lives. Make sure that you use virtual reality in moderation and in a way that does not cause negative effects in your actual life.

## How to Create a CMD Adventure

**Steps**

1. Learn Some Batch. This will be easy; it will only take 5-10 minutes to learn. Again, don't be worried about this step, for Batch is so easy a 10-year-old can learn it.

2. Get a Basic Idea of Your Game. This part is crucial, but pretty easy. Just come up with things like the name of it, genre, etc.

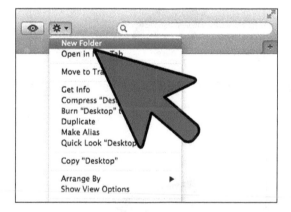

3. Begin. Create a new folder (preferably on your desktop) with the name of your game. Don't use any special characters or spaces, only letters, dashes, and underscores. An example is: "mazes_and_monsters". This way, Command Prompt will be able to open it.

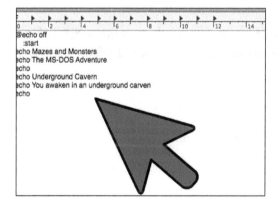

4. Make The First File. Open up Notepad, and write something similar to this:

- `@echo off`

- `:start`

- `echo Mazes and Monsters`

- `echo The MS-DOS Adventure`
- `echo`
- `echo Underground Cavern`
- `echo You awaken in an underground cavern.`
- `echo`

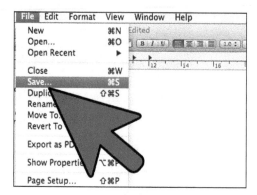

5. After that is done, save it as START.bat, RESTART.bat, etc. and put it in the game file.

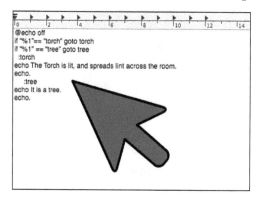

6. Create Commands for Your Game. To do this, make a batch file for each command and place them in the game file. Like EXAMINE.bat. It would look something like this:

- `@echo off`
- `if "%1" == "torch" goto torch`
- `if "%1" == "tree" goto tree`
- `  :torch`
- `echo The torch is lit, and spreads light across the room.`
- `echo.`
- `  :tree`
- `echo It is a tree.`
- `echo.`

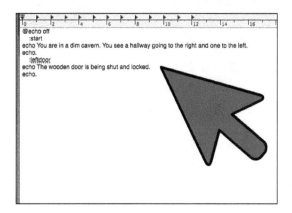

7. "if "%1" == "torch" goto torch" is if they were to enter "examine torch". This does not have to be here. If it is a command that is not used on certain objects, it could look like this:

- `@echo off`

- `:start`

- `echo You are in a dim cavern. You see a hallway going to the right and one to the left.`

- `echo.`

- `:left door`

- `echo The wooden door is barged shut and locked.`

- `echo.`
    - So, if you were to enter that command while you were accessing the :start label, it would show "You are in a dim cavern. You see a hallway going to the right and one to the left," yet if you were to enter "examine" while accessing the :left door label, it would show "The wooden door is barged shut and locked."

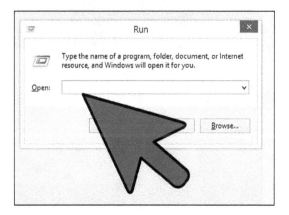

8. Start the Game. Once you're finished with most or the entire game, you'll want to test it. Open Command Prompt, make your way to your game file and open it. Remember when we created the "START.bat" file? We're almost to that. Now, type @echo off, cls, and "start". That will take you to that file, and voila. Try to enter the different commands, test some other things, etc.

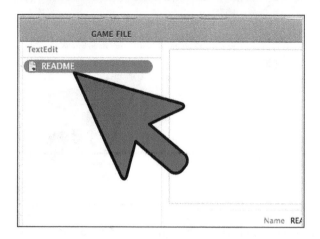

9. Once you near completion, add a README.txt file explaining the game and instructions to starting it in the game file. Then you're ready to go ahead and upload the game file to the World Wide Web.

## How to make a Game Like RuneScape

It might not be the same, but this is how they make it.

### Steps

1. Figure out what you want in your game, make a list with things you really want in your game and put it in a locker until you reach a specific step beneath.

2. Download 3Ds max or buy it (pretty expensive, but do you want new handful updates? Buy it

and you support autodesk) and follow the tutorials. 3Ds max is a very difficult program, but it is used for animations like "Finding Nemo". What you do in 3DS max is you create the models/characters used in the game and so now create a simple character, save it, create an environment, save that, make a turret (enemy that shoots frequently at you, could be an archer/cannon/guy with guns) and save that (all those files should be saved separately).

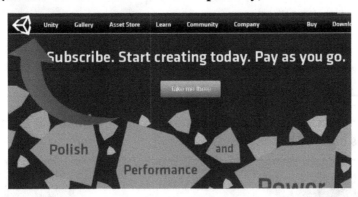

3. Download/buy unity 3D, (this is your engine,) and again follow many tutorials. Create a new scene where you separately load the 3 files and put them together, with a few scripting learned by the tutorials the turret shoots at the character you can steer and attack back.

4. Make a whole world and enemies. This is also the time to pick up your list and scratch things and add them to your game.

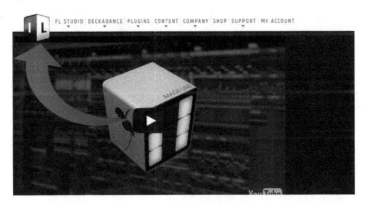

5. Use music software (like fruity loops) to make specific soundtrack. Music could be very important. Do not forget to make trigger sounds like gun sound, walking or shouting.

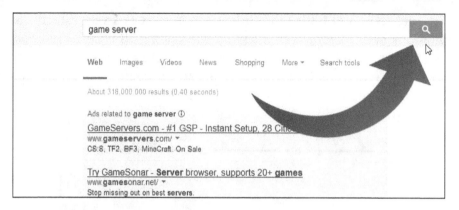

6. Search for a server and create your own website. Do this by making it attractive so you can pay your server payments back with "google ads".

7. Let your game be free. Add attractive extras which the gamers may buy so you can have your profit. Promote your game.

# Software and Tools used for Video Game Development

The choice of design and development tools can help to create an exciting video game. Due to the development atmosphere of virtual reality application and fast-paced gaming environment, there has been tremendous innovation in gaming software and tools. The content in this chapter on making video games with Klik and Play, CMD and Unity 5 will facilitate the understanding of some of the tools and software used for video game development.

## How to make Video Games using Klik and Play

Here is one method of making your own games.

**Steps**

1. Download Klik and Play (KNP). Search Google for Klik and Play download, and download the educational version.

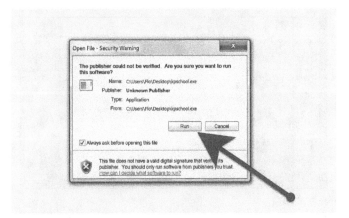

2. Install Klik and Play, then run it.

3. After running KNP, click on "Play Game". and play a few games to see what this engine can create. after you finished, continue to the next step.

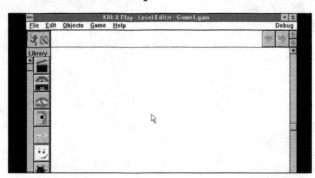

4. Go to the main menu again and click Create Game, now. double-click on the small and empty window and then click Level Editor. This is the engine. Look at the listbox at the left, click one of the objects there. and then click one of the objects in the top listbox.

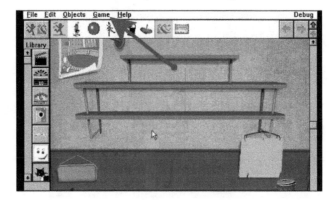

5. Click somewhere in the playground, now. click on the menu called game, now click on Play Level as "Finished". Congratulations. You made a very simple game. Continue experimenting with the engine, and soon you will get the hang of it.

# How to make a Video Game with CMD

## Steps

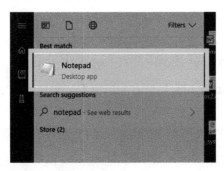

1. Open Notepad. Notepad is a free text editor which is pre-installed on all Windows computers. You'll use Notepad to input your code. To open it, do the following:

- Click Start ▦
- Type in notepad
- Click Notepad at the top of the window.

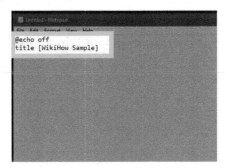

2. Add the title text for your game. Copy the following text into Notepad—making sure to replace "[Title]" with whatever you want to name your game—and then press ↵ Enter:

```
@echo off

title [Title]
```

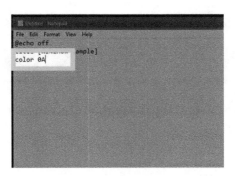

3. Choose a color for your game's text and background. Command Prompt offers several different

colors of text and background which you can trigger by inputting a color-specific code in "0A" format where "0" is the color of the background and "A" is the color of the text. Codes for common colors include the following:

- Text Colors — Use A, B, C, D, E, or F to refer to light-green, light-aqua, light-red, light-purple, light-yellow, or bright-white, respectively.

- Background Colors — Use 0, 1, 2, 3, 4, 5, 6, 7, 8, or 9 to refer to black, blue, green, aqua, red, purple, yellow, white, grey, or light-blue, respectively.

- For example, the standard black-and-white Command Prompt interface would use the code "0F".

4. Set your game's colors. Enter the following text into Notepad—making sure to replace "0A" with your preferred background and text combination—and then press ↵ Enter:

```
@echo off

title OnlineCmag Game

color 0A

if "%1" neq "" ( goto %1)
```

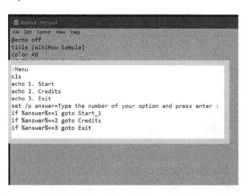

5. Create the game menu. This is essentially the game's startup menu. Enter the following text into Notepad, then press ↵ Enter:

```
:Menu

cls
```

```
echo 1. Start

echo 2. Credits

echo 3. Exit

set /p answer=Type the number of your option and press enter :

if %answer%==1 goto Start_1

if %answer%==2 goto Credits

if %answer%==3 goto Exit
```

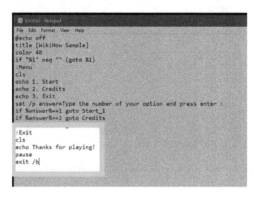

6. Add an "Exit" option. This is how players will be able to exit the Command Prompt. Enter the following text into Notepad, then press ↵ Enter:

```
:Exit

cls

echo Thanks for playing.

pause

exit /b
```

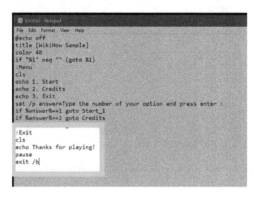

7. Add credits for the game. Enter the following text into Notepad—making sure to replace "[Title]" with your game's title—then press ↵ Enter:

```
:Credits
```

```
cls

echo Credits

echo.

echo Thank you for playing [Title].

pause

goto Menu
```

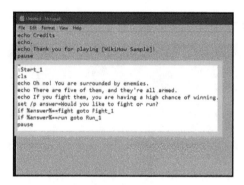

8. Create the "Start" code. This is the code which will allow players to start a new game:

```
:Start_1

cls

echo Oh no. You're surrounded by enemies.

echo There are five of them, and they're all armed.

echo If you fight them, you are having a high chance of winning.

set /p answer=Would you like to fight or run?

if %answer%==fight goto Fight_1

if %answer%==run goto Run_1

pause
```

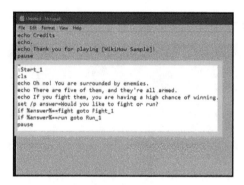

9. Add the action code. Finally, you'll enter the following code to dictate the action of the game:

```
:Run_1

cls

echo You live to fight another day.

pause

goto Start_1

:Fight_1

echo Prepare to fight.

echo The enemies suddenly rush you all at once.

set /p answer= Type 1 and press Enter to continue.

if %answer%==1 goto Fight_1_Loop

:Fight_1_Loop

set /a num=%random%

if %num% gtr 4 goto Fight_1_Loop

if %num% lss 1 goto Fight_1_Loop

if %num%==1 goto Lose_Fight_1

if %num%==2 goto Win_Fight_1

if %num%==3 goto Win_Fight_1

if %num%==4 goto Win_Fight_1

:Lose_Fight_1

cls

echo You were defeated. Play again?

pause

goto Menu

:Win_Fight_1

cls

echo You are victorious.

set /p answer=Would you like to save? [y/n]

if %answer%=='y' goto 'Save'
```

```
if %answer%=='n' goto 'Start_2'

:Save

goto Start_2
```

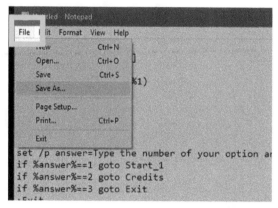

10. Click File. It's in the top-left corner of the Notepad window. A drop-down menu will appear.

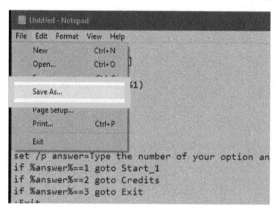

11. Click Save As. It's in the File drop-down menu. Doing so will open a Save As window.

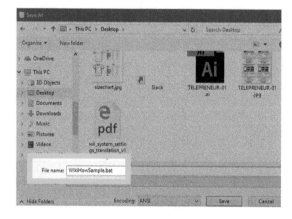

12. Enter a file name followed by the ".bat" extension. In the "File name" text box that's near the bottom of the window, type in whatever you want to name the game followed by.bat to ensure that the game will save as a Command Prompt file.

- For example, to name your game "Dungeon Crawl", you would type in Dungeon Crawl.bat here.

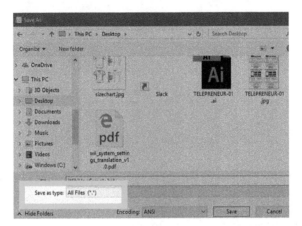

13. Change the file type. Click the "Save as type" drop-down box at the bottom of the window, then click All Files in the resulting drop-down menu.

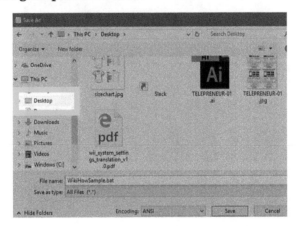

14. Select the desktop as the save location. Click Desktop in the left-hand sidebar to do so. You may first have to scroll up or down on the sidebar in order to find the Desktop folder.

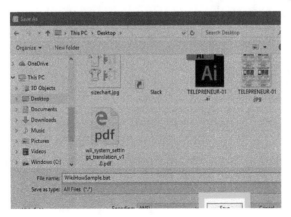

15. Click Save. It's in the bottom-right corner of the window. Doing so will save your game as a BAT file.

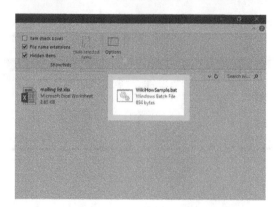

16. Run your game. Double-click the BAT file to open your game in Command Prompt, then follow the on-screen prompts.

- For example, you'll press 1 to start the game.

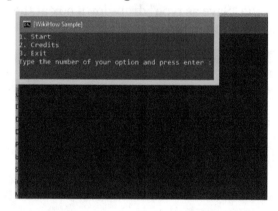

17. Experiment with the code. Now that you have the basic groundwork laid out for the game, you can edit the code to change the in-game text, add options, and more.

- To edit your game's code, right-click the BAT file and then click Edit in the drop-down menu. You can then press Ctrl+S to save any changes.

- Make sure you read through the code to understand what each line of text does.

## How to use Unity 5

Unity 5 is a game engine and development tool used to create video games on computers, consoles, and mobile devices. In this topic, you will learn how to navigate through the Unity interface. Once you are familiarized with the key features and options of Unity, you will be able to start creating your own video games.

### Part 1. Setting Up

1. Install Unity on your computer. Go to https://unity3d.com/ and navigate to the Unity store page. There are three versions of Unity offered. Select the free personal edition option. Check the

box to confirm you have read the terms of service and click "download installer". Once the installer is downloaded, find it in the folder you saved it in and click it to begin installing the program. Make sure you give it permissions when it asks, go through the prompts and select where you want the program to be installed. After that is done, you can begin using Unity.

2. Create a Unity ID. If you do not already have a Unity account, create one by either clicking the prompt, or go to their website. If this is the first time using Unity, the program will ask you to take a short survey.

3. Create a new project. Once you are logged in, the window will show you all the projects on the computer. Since there are none, select the "New" button in the upper right-hand side of the window. Give the project a name, choose where it will be saved, and select whether it is a two dimensional or a three-dimensional project.

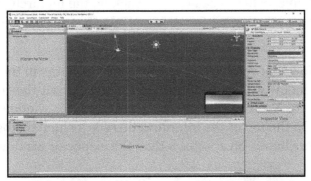

4. Navigate the views. Once the project is made, you are taken to the main Unity screen. Here you will see there are several windows each with different information.

- Scene view – In the center of the Unity window is the scene view. Scenes are basically a level in a game. The scene view window shows all the objects and layout of a room/level. When stating a new project, the only items in the scene are a light source and a camera.

- Hierarchy view – On the left side of the interface, the hierarchy view lists all the items in the current scene. This view allows you to see and select any object in the scene, which makes it much easier to manipulate objects.

- Project view – On the bottom, you will see the project view which is used to navigate through folders of assets for the project. This is how you would organize and access every element used in your game including models, textures, scripts, etc.

- Inspector view – When you have an object in your game selected, you will see all the information of that object in the inspector view. You can also change values and edit objects from this view.

- Game view – By pressing the play button on the top of the screen, Unity will create an instance of your game, and you will be able to play the game or view it through the cameras perspective.

## Part 2. Using Unity

1. Create objects. To add objects to the game, right click on the hierarchy view, hover over the 3D option. A menu will show up listing all the different 3D shapes you can add. For this example, choose the cube shape.

2. Manipulate objects. Now that you have your cube, click its name in the hierarchy window. Notice that the inspector window will show all the information about the cube such as its position, physics, lighting details, etc. You can change the values from this window and they will affect the cube in the scene view. On the top of the interface, there is a small toolbar that will allow you to change objects with a more hands-on approach than the inspector window.

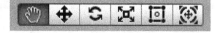

- The hand tool allows you to shift or rotate the scene to change your view. Select this tool, then click and hold on the scene window while moving the cursor around. If you do the same thing while holding down the alt key, you can rotate the scene.

- The Move Tool allows you to select objects and change its position. Select this tool and click on the cube to move it around.

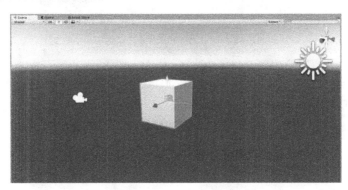

- The Rotate Tool allows you to rotate selected object. When you select this tool and the cube, you should see a sphere around the cube. If you move the lines of the sphere around, you can see that the cube changes its position.

- The Scale Tool lets you change the size of an object. When selected, three pointers how on the cube. If you drag the pointers further from the cube, you will see that the cube extends.

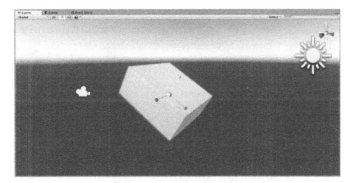

- The Rectangle Tool offers a different way to change the size of an object. When selected, you see four points show up on the cube. Dragging these will change the size of the sides of the cube.

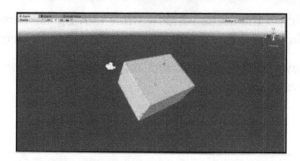

- The last tool on the bar is a combination of the other tools, allowing you to manipulate the cube easily without switching tools.

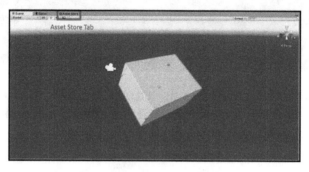

3. Import assets if desired. Aside from making your own objects in the game, you can use items from other sources. You can import your own files, or you may browse the Unity asset store. Select the "asset store" tab at the top of the scene window.

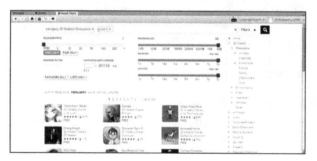

4. Select a model. Once you find the store, you will see the search bar and a menu on the right. Use these to find models that you can use in your game.

5. Download the model. When you find a model you like, just click the blue download button and the files will appear in your project view window.

The Models File

6. Place your model. Return to the scene tab. To put the model into your game, you need to locate its file within the folder you downloaded. You should see a small picture of the model as the icon. Simply drag and drop the icon into the scene view and you can begin working with it.

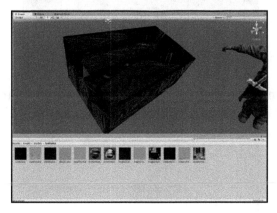

7. Use textures. Just like models, textures can be downloaded from the asset store. They can be placed on models to change how they appear. To demonstrate, I have placed a texture that was in the knights file on our grey cube. Simply drag and drop the texture file onto the block.

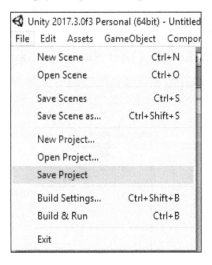

8. Save the project. When you are done working with your project, select file at the top of the screen and click "Save Project". The next time you open Unity, the welcome window will list this project

that you can load and continue to work with. You may also save scenes separately and you may add it to a project later.

## How to Create a Game with Game Maker 7.0 Lite

### Steps

1. Download and install Game Maker 7.0 Lite from http://www.yoyogames.com/gamemaker/windows (the game comes with a simple game called catch the clown that it teaches you how to build)

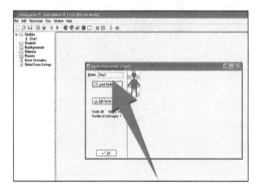

2. Create a new sprite, and load an image of your character. Name it Char1.

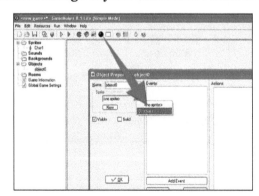

3. Create an object. (click on the blue orb on the tool bar) The sprite for this object should be "Char1."

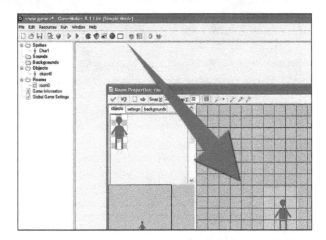

4. Then make a room, (also located on the tool bar) and place your new object inside. In the objects tab of the new room, select char1 and click the main room body to add it.

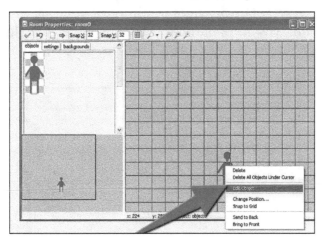

5. Set the object's actions.

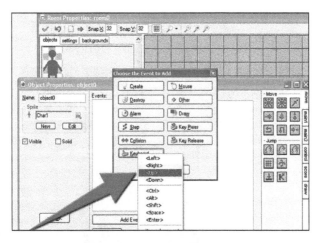

6. Press the add event button and select "arrow keys"(looks like a keyboard, no, not the ones with green or red arrows next to them). For example, select the up key, then in the actions window, put move actions.

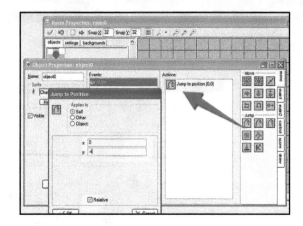

7. To add the actions, go to the move tab and select "jump to Position" not jump to random or anything. Set the parameters(put stuff in the text boxes.) You want to move up right? so in the Y variable textbox, little Y next to it:), put -4. Yes negative, the game works like a backward grid(for those geometry savvy:) Moving right is still positive X and moving left is negative X. Keep the X box at 0. You only want to move up with this key right? No, up. Anyway, Start the game by clicking the play button. If you set this up right, then you should be able to move upwards.

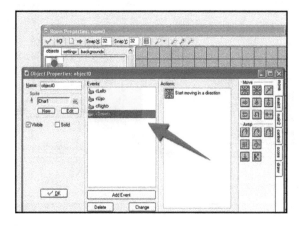

8. Repeat the steps above for all of the other keys, down, right, and left.

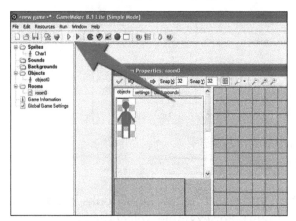

9. Start your game, and you will be able to move around.

# How to Create a Game in RPG Maker XP

The general steps you should be taking if you are interested in creating an RPG (Role-playing Game), specifically in RPG Maker XP, also known as RMXP, a program from the Japanese company Enterbrain.

It's free to download as a trial version for 30 days, or $29.99 USD to purchase. You may notice that the download will come with two items: The RPG maker itself and the RTP (Run-time package) file. The RTP is basically a collection of game materials that the RPG maker needs to run.

Two final notes: First, this guide will not help you get good at the individual steps outlined below. For example, there will be no map-making tips. This guide simply describes the general steps you should take if you're new to the game-making process.

Second, much of the learning process involves figuring things out on your own. There are far too many small intricacies with this program for me to detail here. You will learn quite a bit just by poking around and see what things do, and since it's quite a simple program relatively speaking, you shouldn't feel too overwhelmed.

## Steps

1. Come up with an idea, then flesh it out: Idea creation should always be the first step to any creative endeavor, because you can't reasonably start on it without at least some basis. This also is a step you will probably have the most fun with, considering you likely already have multiple ideas bumping around your head. However, they're probably just small, cool things you want to implement. Flesh these out considerably. Come up with all your characters, environments, enemies, items, weapons, abilities, and anything else you can think of. It will make the actual implementation process far easier if you're working off of a solid outline rather than coming up with things on the fly as you go.

2. Write a script. How much detail you put in is up to you, but having a script, which in this case is both the dialogue that occurs as well as a description of the events, is vital to a well made game. Much like the first step above, getting everything out on paper will give you not only a much better idea of how you're going to go about making the rest of your game, but also make the process far easier, because you'll just be copying and pasting from the script into the dialogue boxes. The script and the document you created in step one will be your most important resources.

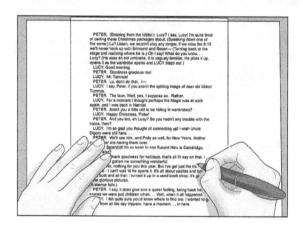

3. Make the map first. The reason for doing map making as your next step is that it will help you to better visualize your world. Doing this will allow you to potentially change your mind about, and fine tune every other aspect of your game. To start creating a map, right click on the first initial map in the map pane, right below the tileset, and click "New Map". You make maps using "tile-sets", which are picture files that have a large variety of different objects and environments within them that are separated by the game maker into a grid. This is because everything you create visually in your game is done as a grid. Each square represents one step a character can take. In these squares, you can place one square of your selected tileset. You can also create events, which will be discussed later. It's also worth mentioning that you can utilize three layers with which to make your map, especially useful for making walls, ceilings, and just anything that you want to be above ground.

You can also edit each square in a tileset to have different characteristics such as the ability to be walked through, and/or from which directions. This is done in the Tilesets tab in the Database, discussed later.

- If you are creating sub-maps that are meant to exist within other maps, for example, a small cave in a forest, make it a sub-map of the forest by right clicking the bigger map and creating the smaller map from that, rather than from the world map. It will make visualizing where maps are that much easier.

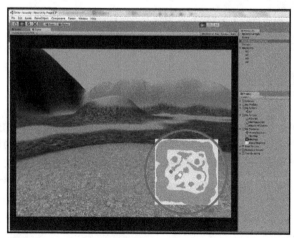

4. Create your game objects. This next section will require much time and fine-tuning as you create

your game. Everything here is done in the Database. The tabs at the top are essentially your to-do list. For the most part, you want to go through each, ensuring that they are filled out with everything your game will contain, from your primary characters, all the weapons, character abilities, item, status effects, monsters, the experience they give, items they drop, and of course, the groups those enemies will be in when they attack your party, as well as editing the different tilesets you have. In other words, create the entire underlay of the game. You also don't have to worry about the "Common Events" or "System" tab just yet. You will be coming back to the Database over and over again as you play through everything you create, but for now, just create the "preliminary draft".

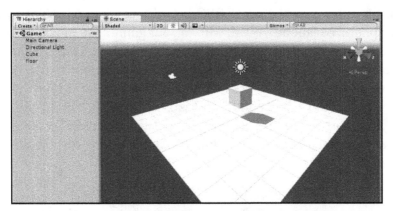

5. Create your events. Here is where the meat of your game creation process lies. To create an event, select the "events" layer. Double click a tile on the map. The options here are immense, but common things you might do are place an NPC (non-playable character, such as a generic village inhabitant) to speak to, cause a conversation to occur between characters, or initiate a battle. You can also cause these events to trigger in multiple ways including upon touch, on clicking the space bar (the default "select" button") next to the tile, or automatically upon entering the map.There is an extremely large variety of customization possible while creating event tiles, and discovering them is part of the fun.

6. Place monsters on the map. You've already created your monster groups, now you have to put them on their respective maps. You can do this in the map menu by right clicking on it in the menu pane, and clicking "Map Properties". There, you'll be able to select which monster groups you want to appear in that map and how common that group will appear.

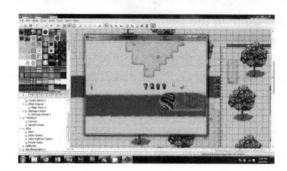

7. Choose your music: What would a great RPG be without its music? The music in your game provides the "atmospheric backbone", if you will, to your game. The music you choose will be part of the memories those who play your game will associate with it. You can choose any music you want, from the included tracks or an MP3 file of your choosing, for maps, battles, boss battles, cinematics, everything. They essentially create the mood, so be sure to take the tone of the current in-game situation into account when choosing. Map music is chosen on the map menu you set your monster groups in, battle music is set in the Database, as is music for common things in every game like the title screen and game over screen. You can also set a certain song to play whenever you want using an event.

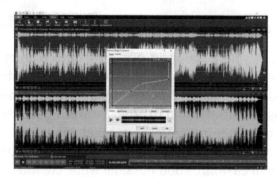

8. Add side-quests. This step is technically optional, but is heavily recommended. Sure, the main storyline is the important part, but everyone loves some good sidequests. They go a long way into making your game less linear. Some ideas might be killing an optional monster to get a sweet weapon, completing a special dungeon with a large sum of money at the end, or anything really that you can think of.

9. Playtest, playtest, playtest. You should not only be testing sections and battles repeatedly, but also the entire game, because maintaining a good balance (i.e. difficulty level) and engaging experience is vital. A good thing to do is have a main save file that you're going through the game with,

and then you can adjust battles for what a normal party would be at for that stage in the game. Make sure to go through everything with a fine-toothed comb because bugs are everywhere, and very easy to miss. Not only that, but they can be potentially game-breaking, such as a door you are unable to go through to advance the plot. So make sure you play through your game multiple times until it's perfect. Congratulations, you're done your game. However, you want people to play it don't you?

10. Distribution. When you finally finish your game and want others to play it, you have several options. The first and easiest way, assuming one of these people is a friend of yours, if to just get them to play on the computer you made the game on and just play through it in the RMXP program itself. However, if you want to actually be able to put the file onto a disk to give it to someone to play, it's an easy process.

- Compress the game data: Go to "File" and then click "Compress game data". It will ask for a destination folder (or disk). This compressed data has all the information the game needs to run except for the audio files and graphics. This comes back to what I mentioned at the beginning regarding the RTP. If the person using your game has installed the RTP file on their own computer, then they can simply run the game off of this compressed game file. Having RMXP installed is not needed for them.

- To download the RTP file separately, go here: http://www.rpgmakerweb.com/download/run-time-package

- If they don't have it installed, you will need to include the audio and graphics folders along with the compressed data, which will make the file you're sending much bigger. When your recipient wants to run the game, they just need to double-click the "Game" file.

The image shown below are from RPG Maker VX Ace, not RPG Maker XP. The are just there to illustrate the points. The interfaces and are similar enough that it's roughly the same.

## How to Create an FPS Creator Game

### Steps

1. Buy FPS Creator.

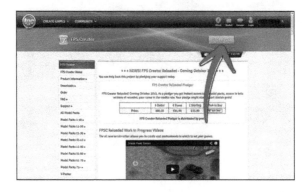

2. Install FPS Creator.

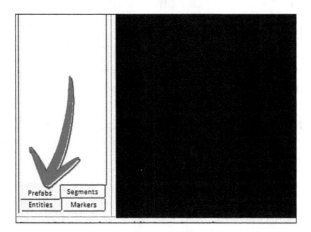

3. If you already own the software, you could set up rooms with segments, but if you have only just bought the game, select the prefab section.

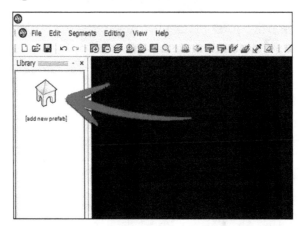

4. Click "Add New Prefab".

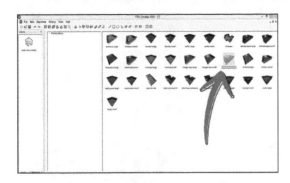

5. Pick a building that you want in game and click "OK".

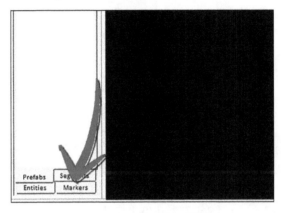

6. Select the "Markers" tab just below the section where you clicked "Add New Prefab".

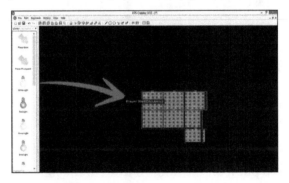

7. Select a "Player Start" and put it where you want the player to start (R is rotate).

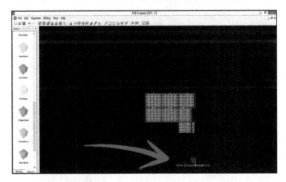

8. Select a Win Zone and put it where you want the game to end.

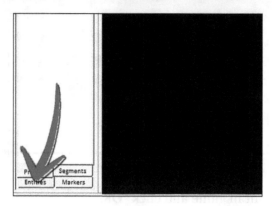

9. Select the "Entities" tab and click "Add new entity".

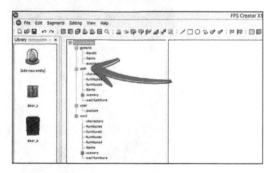

10. Go into either the "Items" under "Sci-Fi" or "WW2".

11. Pick a gun to fight with and put it on the floor in front of the player start (make sure it is in front of where the arrow is pointing).

12. Click "Add new entity" again and this time select "Characters" under "Sci-Fi" or "WW2" and pick your character for the game.

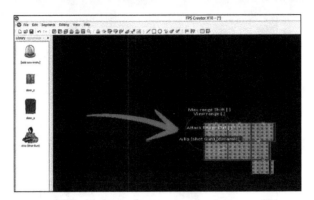

13. Put the character in the game.

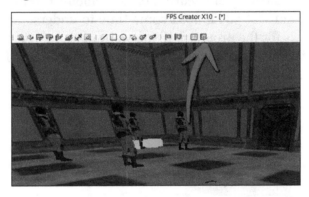

14. Push the green "Test Game" button and watch your game intelligently react.

## How to make a Game using Construct 2

### Method 1. Basic Things

1. Download Construct 2: To begin with, Construct 2 is a 2D game engine that is 100% programming free, to test it you can download the free edition but if you really like it, you can buy the license for full version.

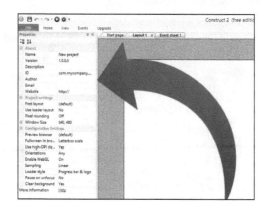

2. Explore the program: See the program, learn it basic elements & try to configure this thing out. It's a well organized program, but you'll need some time to understand all of it. Here's a photo show you the main windows for the program. If you want more info & lean faster you can see the manual of Construct2, it is downloaded with the program files with lot of example projects so you can understand it quickly.

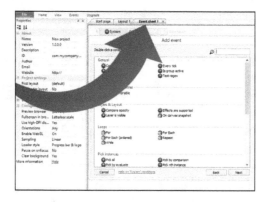

3. Learn the event system: The game engine is 100% codes free, but you will need to know the basic of the event system Construct 2 uses. It's a simple logic system that consists of conditions & actions. When a condition is true, the wanted action is triggered. You will need weeks to get well skilled at knowing events system, but it's easy and you will just need to practice a lot.

## Method 2. Online Things

1. Join Scirra's Community. Scirra is the Developer Company of construct 2. It's consists of two

mainly people: Ashley & Tom Gullen. Once you have an account on Scirra's website you can access to many things like: Tutorials, Scirra arcade, Blog, and forums. Scirra Website. Tutorials are written by construct 2 experienced users so you can refer to it because the manual can give you everything. Scirra arcade is an online arcade for games done & published by construct 2 users. You can upload your game there if you want. Scirra's Blog is blog made by Scirra's team to announce latest changes in construct 2 or extra features. The forum is used by construct 2 users to post stuff, you can also ask help from others by posting in the forum or you can send Private message to any online user.

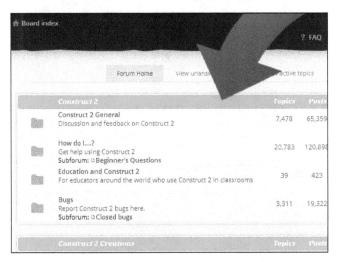

2. Get help from others. If you feel stuck or confused you can ask any one online on the forum or you can also send private messages to do this follow here: Scirra Forums Note: you must be a registered user before you can post to get help.

3. Be successful. You need to focus on one game category so you can excel in it. Find a game category that you mostly like and if you said you like all of them you can choose a category that is less threatening to you. To know more about categories and how to make a successful game click here: How to make a successful game This steps will make you right on track.

## Method 3. Extra Things

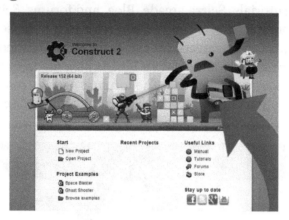

1. Be creative: Being game developer is not an easy task it need skills & time. If you are willing to make games you must be creative to do it.

2. Play games: if you want to be a game maker we must be a gamer. Try to play usually and play a lot of them. As you play different games as you get ideas and concepts for your games.

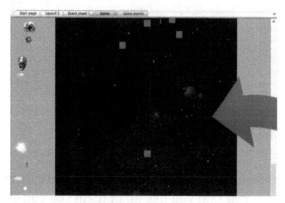

3. Practice a lot: You need to use construct 2 all the time , to learn faster make game projects and have fun as you do them, it's not attempt to make a game, it just a practice for it, so don't make game first, just get experiences and lot of small projects.

# How to Create Pong in Unity 2017

Unity Engine is a game development engine aimed at making games easier to develop. For many beginners, especially those without coding experience, the idea of creating a video game can seem like a daunting task, but with a development engine like Unity that process can be made much easier.

## Part 1. Creating the Project

1. Start a new project by clicking "New" on the Unity Projects tab.

2. Name the project, and ensure the box "2D" is checked. Then click the "Create Project" button in the bottom right corner.

## Part 2. Exploring the Unity Editor

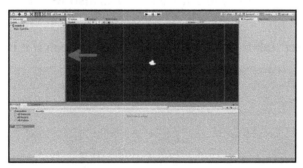

1. Review the left side. This is the current scene you're looking at as well as what game objects are in the scene. Currently the scene is named "Untitled" and the only object in it is the "Main Camera". This area is also referred to as the "Hierarchy".

2. Click on the Camera in the Hierarchy to select it. This will highlight it in blue.

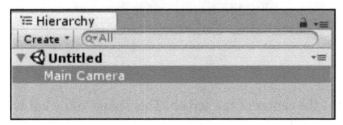

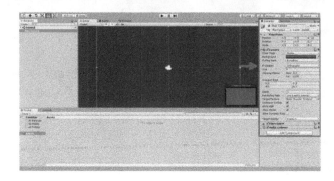

3. Find the inspector. The right side of the screen is the inspector, and this shows you the properties of game objects you're selecting. The "main camera" is currently selected, hence the fact that it's highlighted in blue in the hierarchy on the left, so the inspector shows the properties of the main camera.

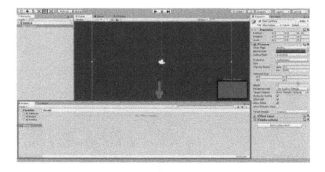

4. Review the asset folder and console, at the bottom. This is where all of the assets in the game (cameras, scenes, scripts, etc.) are stored. This is also where you can import files to use in unity.

- Click on the "Project" tab to ensure the asset folder is open if it isn't already.

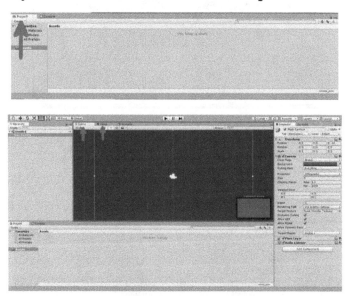

5. Find the scene view at the center of the screen. This shows you what is currently in the scene,

and you can toggle between the scene view and the game view using the buttons the arrows are pointing to.

- Right above the scene view there are the buttons that allow you to play the scene and pause the scene to see what it would look like for a normal player.

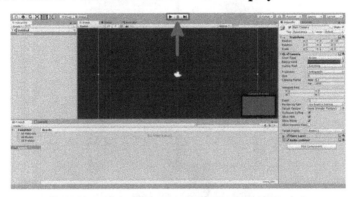

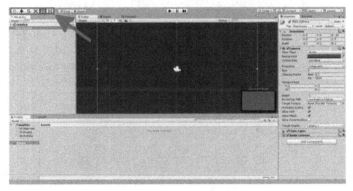

6. Find the manipulator buttons. Finally, in the upper left corner you can see different options that allow you to manipulate the scene, and objects in it in different ways.

## Part 3. Creating Player 1

1. Create Player 1. To start, download the sprite by clicking here.

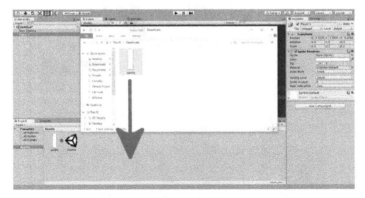

2. Import the sprite into the asset folder. Find where the image has been saved on your computer, and drag it from that folder into the asset folder inside of the Unity Editor.

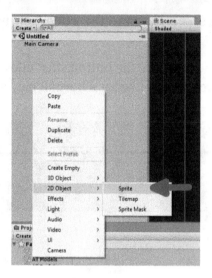

3. Right click inside of the hierarchy and go to 2D Object, and create a Sprite.

- Ensure the created sprite isn't a child of the Main Camera. If there's a drop down arrow next to the camera you've accidentally make the sprite a child of the main camera. Try to ensure that nothing in the hierarchy is like this.

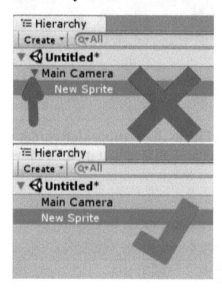

- If it is a child simply grab the Sprite and drag it down a bit inside of the hierarchy. This will unchild it.

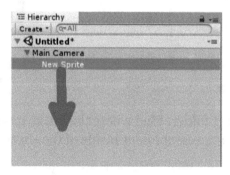

4. Click on the object we've just created you can see information about it. This area is called the inspector, and this is where you can modify some things about the object. Firstly rename it to "Player 1".

5. Set the position of the object to (0, 0, 0). Sometimes objects will start with transform values that may place them off screen, so be sure to check that when creating new objects.

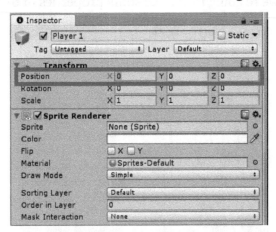

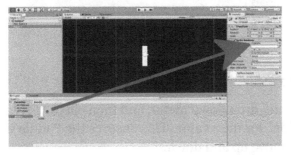

6. Apply the sprite to the Sprite Renderer of on Player 1. Click on player 1 in the scene, and drag the

sprite from the asset folder to the "sprite" box on the Sprite Render component in the inspector.

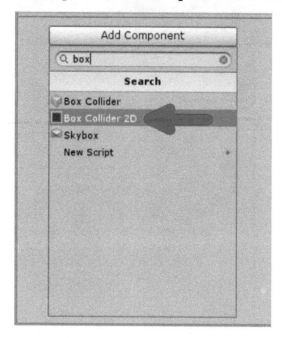

7. Add a Box Collider 2D to the Paddle. Click "Add Component" and search for "Box Collider 2D", Make sure this is the 2D version , and not simply the Box Collider.

8. Add a Rigidbody 2D using the same process. Click "Add Component" and search for "Rigidbody 2D". Now in the inspector we're going to change some properties of the Rigidbody.

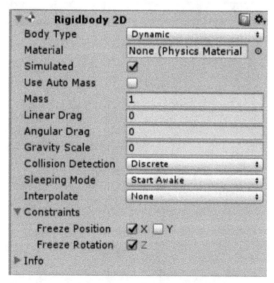

- Change the "Gravity Scale" to 0. This ensures the paddle won't be affected by gravity.

- Click the "Constraints" drop down menu, and then check "Freeze Position" for the x value, and "Freeze Rotation" for the z value. This ensures the Paddle will only move in the Y axis, or simply will only move up and down.

## Part 4. Writing the Paddle Code

1. Create the script that controls the Paddles behavior. Right click in the Asset menu at the bottom, and go to *Create > C# Script*. Name the script "Paddle" so it's easy to keep track of it.

```csharp
using System.Collections;
using System.Collections.Generic;
using UnityEngine;

public class Paddle : MonoBehaviour {


    // Use this for initialization
    void Start () {

    }

    // Update is called once per frame
    void Update () {

    }
}
```

2. Double click on the newly created script to open it.

- Inside of the C# Script you should have a blank project.

```csharp
using System.Collections;
using System.Collections.Generic;
using UnityEngine;

public class Paddle : MonoBehaviour {

    public KeyCode up;
    public KeyCode down;
    Rigidbody2D rigidBody;

    // Use this for initialization
    void Start () {

    }
}
```

3. Type code above the Start() function that declares the up and down arrows, and how to move the player.

- public KeyCode up;
- public KeyCode down;

- Rigidbody2D rigidBody;

- The up and down are keys that you will set later to move the paddle up and down. Rigidbody2D is what you modify to allow the player to move.

- When you type new code a yellow bar will appear on the side. This shows what code was recently added to the script, and will go away once you save the script.

```
 0 references
5    public class Player : MonoBehaviour {
6
7        public KeyCode up;
8        public KeyCode down;
9        Rigidbody2D rigidBody;
10
11       // Use this for initialization
     0 references
12       void Start () {
```

```
1    using System.Collections;
2    using System.Collections.Generic;
3    using UnityEngine;
4
5    public class Paddle : MonoBehaviour {
6
7        public KeyCode up;
8        public KeyCode down;
9        Rigidbody2D rigidBody;
10
11       // Use this for initialization
12       void Start () {
13           rigidBody = GetComponent<Rigidbody2D>();
14       }
15
```

4. Tell the Rigidbody variable to find the "Rigidbody" that was attached to the paddle earlier. Type rigidBody = GetComponent<Rigidbody2D>(); inside of the start function.

```
15
16       // Update is called once per frame
17       void Update () {
18           if(Input.GetKey(up))
19           {
20               rigidBody.velocity = new Vector2(0f, 7f);
21           }
22           else if (Input.GetKey(down))
23           {
24               rigidBody.velocity = new Vector2(0f, -7f);
25           }
26           else
27           {
28               rigidBody.velocity = new Vector2(0f, 0f);
29           }
30       }
31   }
32
```

5. Type the following into the update function.

```
if(input.GetKey(up))

{

    rigidBody.velocity = new Vector2(0f, 7f);

}

else if(input.GetKey(down))

{
```

```
    rigidBody.velocity = new Vector2(0f, 7f);

}

else

{

    rigidBody.velocity = new Vector2(0f, 0f);

}
```

- This will tell the paddle how it's supposed to move when you press up or down. Basically, if the player presses the "up" button they will move up 7 units per second, if they press "down" they will move down 7 units per second, and if they press nothing they wont move.

6. Press Ctrl+S to save the script,. Head back into the Unity Editor by either tabbing back, or closing Visual Studio.

## Part 5. Creating Player 2

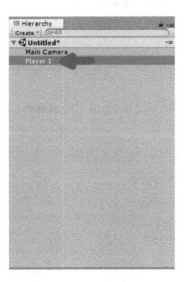

1. Select the Player 1 Game Object in the scene by clicking on it inside of the hierarchy.

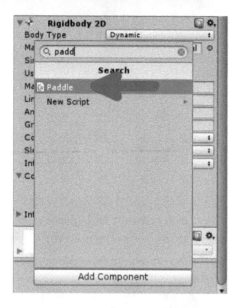

2. Apply the Player script to the Player 1 Game Object. Click "Add component" on Player 1, and search for the name of the player script. In this case the name is "Paddle".

- You could also click and drag the script from the asset menu to the Inspector on the right.

3. Select the Player 1 paddle. Under the "Paddle" component in the inspector, there should be a drop down menu to select up or down. Choose the keys you wish to make the player move up or down. For this example the "W" and "S" keys are used.

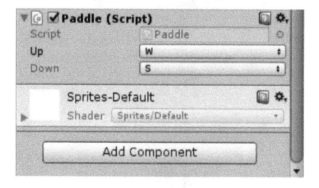

4. Move the player more towards the left side of the screen. Click on Player 1 in the scene, and change the X value in the position to -8.

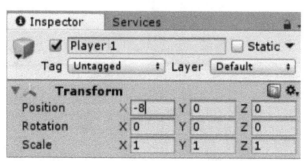

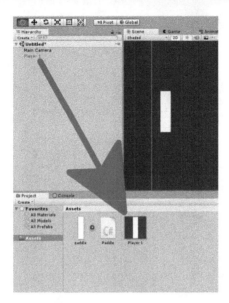

5. Create Player 2 by making the current player into what is called a Prefab. To do this you're going to select it in the scene, and drag it down to the asset panel. This will create the prefab.

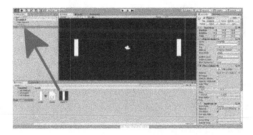

6. Drag that prefab back into the scene. Now you've made a clone of Player 1, except this clone can take on different values if you want it to.

7. Rename the new object to "Player 2". Change its x value to a positive 8, and set the keys to move this object in the same way you did previously, this time using the up and down arrows.

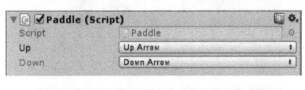

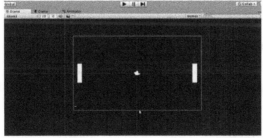

8. Press the play button at the top. You can see the game run, and you have two different objects that can move with different keys.

## Part 6. Creating the Play Area

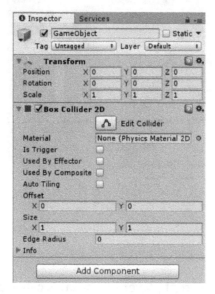

1. Right click on the scene. Click on "Create Empty" now add a Box Collider 2D to the object.

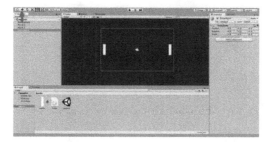

2. Move the object so it's more towards the top of the screen. Select the move tool in the upper left.

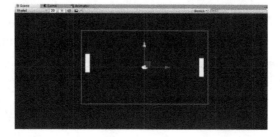

3. Click on the green arrow on the game object. Drag it towards the top to create the upper wall.

4. Click "Edit Collider" to change the boundaries so they cover all the area from the left and right paddle.

- When you click off of the Wall in the hierarchy, the outline for the green wall will disappear, but don't worry, it's still there; it just doesn't display it unless it's selected.

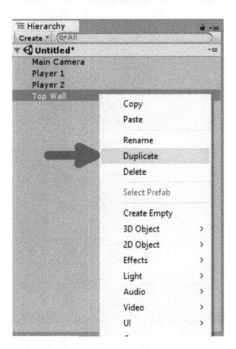

5. Right click on the top wall in the hierarchy, and click duplicate. Then drag it down so underneath the paddles, so that it serves as the bottom wall.

- Finally, this is how it should look.

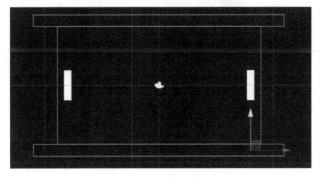

## Part 7. Creating the Ball

1. Create the ball that you'll hit back and forth. Download the sprite for the ball here.

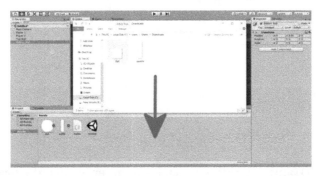

2. Import the downloaded sprite into the Unity Editor.

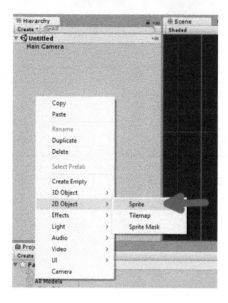

3. Right click in the hierarchy, and create a sprite. Rename this sprite to "Ball".

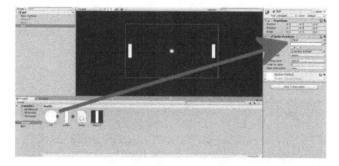

4. Apply the imported sprite to the game object.

5. Add a Circle Collider 2D, and a Rigidbody 2D. Remember to turn the gravity scale to 0, and angular drag to 0, and finally set the rotation in the z axis to be locked.

6. Create a physics material for the ball. This is what will allow it to bounce off the walls. Right click in the asset folder, and go to "Create Physics Material 2D"

7. Name the material something like "Bounce." Set the friction to 0 and the bounciness to 1. This will ensure it never loses velocity.

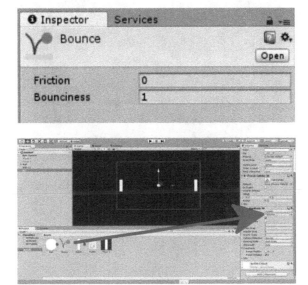

8. Apply the material to the Rigid body of the ball game object.

## Part 8. Creating the Ball Code

1. Right click in the asset folder, and go to *Create > C# Script*. Name the script "Ball". Now double click on that script to open it.

```
Rigidbody2D rigidBody;

// Use this for initialization
void Start () {
    rigidBody = GetComponent<Rigidbody2D>();
}
```

2. Type Rigidbody2D rigidBody; above the start function, and rigidBody = GetComponent<Rigidbody2D>(); inside the Start() function.

- This gives us access to the balls Rigidbody, which will allow us to apply force to it.

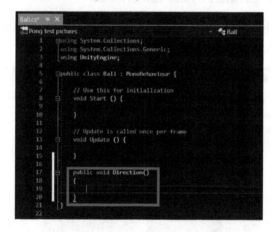

3. Create a function that will set the ball'ss velocity. Type the following underneath the "Start()" and "Update()" functions.

```
public void Direction()

{


}
```

```
public void Direction()
{
    int direction;
    direction = Random.Range(0, 2);
    if(direction == 0)
    {
        rigidBody.velocity = new Vector2(5f, -3f);
    }
    else
    {
        rigidBody.velocity = new Vector2(-5f, 3f);
    }
}
```

4. Type the following inside of the newly created Direction() function:

```
int direction;
```

```
direction = Random.Range(0, 2);

if(direction == 0)

{

    rigidBody.velocity = new Vector2(5f, -3f);

}

else

{

    rigidBody.velocity = new Vector2(-5f, 3f);

}
```

- This is what the function Random.Range will do for you, by generating a random number either 0 or 1. Then it will give the ball a velocity of either (5, -3) or (-5, 3) depending.

5. Add Direction() to the balls "Start()" function. This will cause it to trigger when the game starts.

```
// Use this for initialization
void Start () {
    rigidBody = GetComponent<Rigidbody2D>();
    Direction();
}
```

```
 3    using UnityEngine;
 4
 5    public class Ball : MonoBehaviour {
 6
 7        Rigidbody2D rigidBody;
 8
 9        // Use this for initialization
10        void Start () {
11            rigidBody = GetComponent<Rigidbody2D>();
12            Direction();
13        }
14
15        // Update is called once per frame
16        void Update () {
17
18        }
19
20        public void Direction()
21        {
22            int direction;
23            direction = Random.Range(0, 2);
24            if(direction == 0)
25            {
26                rigidBody.velocity = new Vector2(5f, -3f);
27            }
28            else
29            {
30                rigidBody.velocity = new Vector2(-5f, 3f);
31            }
32        }
33    }
34
```

6. Press Ctrl+S to save the script. Head back to the Unity Editor.

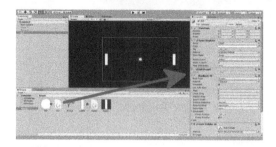

7. Apply the Ball script to the Ball game object. Select the ball in the hierarchy, and then drag the Ball script from the assets folder onto the Ball in the inspector.

## Part 9. Creating the Goals

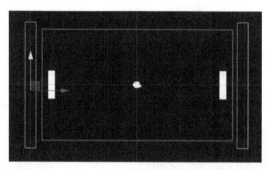

1. Right click, *Create > Empty*, and apply a Box Collider 2D to the object you just created. Set them up a bit behind the paddles, and ensure that they cover from the top wall to the bottom wall on both sides

2. Check the "Is Trigger" box under "Box Collider 2D". This allows us to have something happen when an object enters that trigger. In this case it will reset the ball to the center.

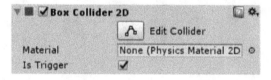

## Part 10. Creating the Goal Code

1. Right click in the asset folder, and click *Create > C# Script*. Rename the script to "Goal" Double click on the newly created script to open it.

```
void OnTriggerEnter2D(Collider2D collider)
{
    //This resets the ball to the initial position
    collider.transform.position = new Vector2(0f, 0f);
    //This causes the ball to choose a random direction
    collider.GetComponent<Ball>().Direction();
}
```

2. Type the following under the Start() function:

```
void OnTriggerEnter2D(Collider2D collider)

{

    collider.GetComponent<Ball>().Direction();

    collider.transform.position = new Vector2(0f, 0f);

}
```

- "collider.transform.position = new Vector2(0f, 0f);" is how the ball gets set back to the initial position. The collider in this case being the ball.

- "collider.GetComponent<Ball>().Direction();" gets the Direction function on the ball when it passes through, and makes sure it runs again.

- So essentially the ball returns to the center and once again chooses a random direction.

3. Press Ctrl+Sto save the script. Then head back to the Unity Editor.

4. Attach the script to both goals by using "Add component" in the inspector.

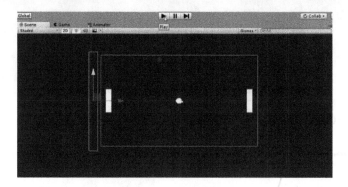

5. Press Play and witness the finished project.

6. Go to *File* > *Save* project so that you can keep your project forever.

## How to make Video Games with Unreal Engine 4

Learn how to make video games using the industry-leading game development software, Unreal Engine 4. Learn game development and design with no programming experience required.

1. Register an account with Epic Games. Go to https://unrealengine.com and click the blue "Get Unreal" button in the upper-right corner. Fill out the registration form, then click the "Sign Up" button. If you agree with the End User License Agreement, then accept it to proceed.

2. Download and install Unreal Engine 4.

- Click the Download button and open the.msi file that downloads.

- Choose a folder path and click "Install" to install the Epic Games Launcher.

- Run the Epic Games Launcher and login using the registration info you provided when you registered your account.

- Click the yellow button that says "Install Engine".

- Accept the EULA to download and install Unreal Engine 4.

- Click the yellow button that says "Launch" to run the Unreal Engine.

3. Create a new project. A project, in the context of UE4, is a file used to store all the data for each game you are developing. When you open UE4, the first thing it will do is launch the Unreal Project Browser.

- In the "Projects" tab, you can open your existing projects. In the "New Project" tab, you can create a new blank project or a new project based on a template. To create a new project, make your selections, then click on the green "Create Project" button in the bottom-right.

4. Create a new level. A level, in the context of the Unreal Engine, is an area where gameplay occurs. To create, open, or save a level, use the File Menu.

- To test a level directly in the Level Editor, use the play button in the toolbar at the top of the screen. To enter or exit full screen mode, use the F11 key.

## Part 1. Using Actors

1. Understand actors. An actor, in the Unreal Engine, is any object that has been added to a level.

- For example, find the cube in the menu on the left side of the screen. Click on it, then drag-and-drop it into the window in the middle. The cube in the middle window is now an actor within the level.

- Note that not all actors are physical objects. For example, there are several actors that simply mark specific places in a Level where certain things should occur. These are still actors even though players will never see them in the game.

2. Know how meshes affect your actors. Mesh is a 3D-modeling term that refers to visible 3D objects. Unreal Engine has two main types of mesh actors - the static mesh actor and the skeletal mesh actor.

- The static mesh actor is for meshes with no moving parts.

- The skeletal mesh actor is for meshes that do having moving parts.

- The starter content contains some meshes you can use but third-party 3D-modeling programs, such as Maya, 3D Studio Max, or Blender, create most meshes used in games. You can find lots of meshes for free and for sale in the Epic Games Launcher and on the Internet in general.

3. Know the difference between brushes and meshes. Brushes, also known as geometry brushes, are actors that model 3D space. This is very close to the definition of a mesh, but there are some key differences between the two.

- Brushes are for simpler shapes while meshes are for more complex shapes. Brushes are easier to work with but require more memory. So, in general, use brushes to quickly prototype the layouts of levels, and then replace them with meshes for the final product. You can access brushes from the Geometry tab on the left side of the Editor.

4. Get to know the materials. The material of an actor is a property that is common to both meshes and brushes. A material is an asset you can apply to the surfaces of Actors to make those actors appear to be made out of that material. For example, you could apply a wood material to a cube mesh to make a "wooden cube."

5. Understand how light works. The purpose of a light actor is to represent visible light. Note that they only represent the light itself and not the object from which the light emanates. For example, to have a lamp in your level, you would need a static mesh actor of a lamp, including the light bulb, in addition to a light actor in the same location as the bulb. There are four types of light actors in Unreal:

- Directional Light Actor - used to mimic light coming from an extremely long distance away, such as outer space; used primarily for sunlight and moonlight.

- Point Light - for light that emanates in all directions, like from a light bulb, or fire.

- Spot Light - emits light in the shape of a cone, like from a flashlight, or, as the name suggests, a spot light.

- Sky Light Actor - emulates the light that reflects off the atmosphere (the "glow" of the atmosphere).

## Part 2. Using the Level Editor

1. Know the panels of the Level Editor. The Level Editor is the home screen when developing games in the Unreal Engine application. The large rectangle in the middle is the viewport. The thin strip above that is the toolbar. At the bottom of the screen is the content browser. On the left side of the screen is the modes panel. On the right side of the screen is the world outliner at the top, and below that, the details panel.

2. Use mouse navigation. To use mouse navigation, hold down one of the following mouse buttons or button combinations and drag the mouse to perform the action:

- LMB - move forward or backwards, rotate left or right

- LMB+RMB / MMB - move left, right, up, or down

- RMB - rotate in any direction

3. Use WASD navigation. To use WASD navigation, keep the RMB held down the entire time: Maya refers to a popular 3D-modeling program that uses these controls. To use Maya navigation, keep the Alt key held down, then hold one of the following mouse buttons and drag the mouse:

- Drag the mouse - rotate in any direction

- W, A, S, D keys - forward, left, backwards, right

- Q and E keys - up, down

- Z and C keys - zoom in and out

4. Use Maya navigation. Maya refers to a popular 3D-modeling program that uses these controls. To use Maya navigation, keep the Alt key held down, then hold one of the following mouse buttons and drag the mouse:

- LMB - tumble/orbit the camera around a single point of interest

- RMB - dolly/zoom the camera towards and away from a point of interest

- MMB - track/pan the camera up, down, left, and right

5. Move, rotate, and scale actors. To move, rotate, and scale actors in the Level Editor, use the Move, Rotate, and Scale Tools. You can see which tool is selected by looking at the first three icons in the upper-right of the viewport.

- To switch between the tools, click their icons, or use the shortcut keys W, E, and R.

- When the Move Tool is selected, three colored arrows will appear on the currently selected actor. To move an actor along a particular axis, click on the corresponding arrow and drag the mouse. To move an actor in two dimensions, click on the connector between the arrows. For all three dimensions at once, click on the white sphere in the middle of the arrows.

- When the Rotate Tool is selected, you can rotate an actor around one of the three axes by clicking on one of the colored arcs and dragging the mouse.

- When the Scale Tool is selected, you can make your actors bigger or smaller. Just like with the Move Tool, you can manipulate the actor in one, two, or three dimensions at a time.

6. Use the details panel. When an actor is selected, the details panel will display the properties of that actor, most of which can be edited.

- The transform category is common to all actors. In the transform category, you can move, rotate, and scale actors manually by entering values directly. This is useful when you need precision or exact values.

- Mobility is a setting that applies primarily to mesh actors and light actors. For meshes, there are two options - static and moveable. Static means the actor will remain in place the entire time, while moveable means it's possible for the actor's location to change. For light actors, there is a third option - stationary. This is used for lights that don't move, but can change in other ways such as changing color or turning on or off.

## Part 3. Making Blueprints

1. Understand blueprints. A blueprint in the Unreal Engine is an asset that contains data and instructions. With blueprints, you specify the logic that controls your games and keeps track of important data such as health, energy, score, etc.

2. Understand the difference between level blueprints and blueprint classes. There are two main types of blueprints, the level blueprint and blueprint classes.

- A level blueprint holds data and instructions for a particular level. It might hold data such as the time remaining to complete the Level, or the number of keys you've collected in that level, and so on. It also stores instructions that pertain only to that level.

- Blueprint classes are a way to turn any actor or asset into a blueprint. This allows you to create objects with custom traits and behaviors. One of the great things about blueprint classes is that you can use them to create as many copies, or instances, of your creation as you want. Once you complete a blueprint class, it will be available to you in the content browser, and each time you drag it into the viewport, it will create a new instance of that actor. Each instance has its own data independent from the other instances.

3. Get to know the Level Blueprint Editor. To open a level blueprint, go to the toolbar, click the blueprints button, then click on "Open Level Blueprint." This will open the Level Blueprint Editor. Inside the Level Blueprint Editor is the event graph.

- The event graph is where you script logic. If you're a programmer, you can script the logic in pure code using C++. However, Epic Games has a visual scripting system that allows non-programmers to script logic and can be convenient even for programmers with experience.

4. Understand nodes. The scripting system works by using various nodes, that each serve a specific purpose, and connecting those nodes together. By default, the level blueprint starts off with two commonly used nodes in the graph. They are disabled to start with, but can be used right away by connecting them to another node.

- The first node is the Event BeginPlay Node. An event node is a node that activates when a certain event occurs. So an Event BeginPlay Node, inside of a level blueprint, will be activated by the event of the level first starting.

- The second default node is also an event node. The Event Tick Node is a node that activates on every tick of gameplay. Before every frame of the game draws on the screen, any logic that connects to the Event Tick Node will execute. This is useful in situations where you need to constantly check certain conditions that, when met, will have an immediate effect on the game, such as the main character colliding with something harmful.

5. Locate and understand the pins and wires. The icons along the left and/or right sides of nodes are pins. Pins on the left side of a node are input pins and pins on the right side of a node are output pins. They input/output data to and from nodes and specify the order in which Nodes should execute. Pins connect to one another with wires.

- To create a wire, left-click on a pin and then drag the mouse while still holding the LMB. This will drag a wire out of that pin. If you hover over another pin and release the LMB, it will connect the end of the wire to that pin.

- Pins with a white icon that looks like a play button are execution pins. Execution pins on the left side of a node are input execution pins. When a wire connected to an input execution pin activates, it will trigger execution of that node. Execution pins on the right side of a node are output execution pins. Wires connected to an output execution pin will activate once that node has finished executing. Output execution pins can only connect to input execution pins and vice-versa.

- By chaining nodes together through their execution pins, you can define a series of nodes that should execute, one after the other, every time the first node in the series activates. The first node in a chain will always be an event node.

- Pins with a circular icon are data pins. The purpose of data pins is to pass data between nodes. Output data pins can only connect to input data pins and vice-versa. Whatever data the output data pin contains is sent to the input data pin it connects to.

6. Add nodes. To add a new node to the event graph, you will need to select that node from the node menu. The node menu is brought up by right-clicking on any empty space in the graph, or by releasing the LMB over any empty space when dragging out a wire from an output execution pin. When doing the latter, the node you add will automatically connect to the wire.

- There are many nodes available to choose from in the node menu. They are organized into categories, but if you know at least part of the name of the node you're looking for, you can use the search box at the top of the node menu to search for it.

## How to Create a Game Like Club Penguin in Game Maker 8

If you have ever played a game like Club Penguin, or know someone that has, then maybe you've wondered how to make a game like that. You can use Game Maker.

### Steps

1. Download Game Maker from yoyogames.com for free. This will be the free version. You can purchase the Pro Edition of Game Maker at a low price

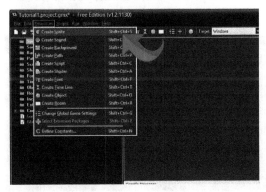

2. Now it's time to start creating your game. The best way to start that is by creating sprites, which are basically images. You can use MS Paint or most any art program that you want (Game Maker

comes with one also). This is the main part of creating your game, since it shows how much quality your game has. If you're not that good at drawing, you can always create your sprites by getting images from the Internet. If this is your first time creating a game, start simple and don't go overboard. In Club Penguin, the main characters are penguins, but you can do any characters that you want, whether they are animals or people.

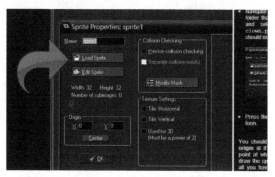

3. Upload your pictures into Game Maker 8. Now that that is done, we can start creating our objects. To have your characters move, you could program it so that they move when the player presses the arrow keys. Start this by creating an event. To have an object do what you want it to do, browse through the events, and then through the commands.

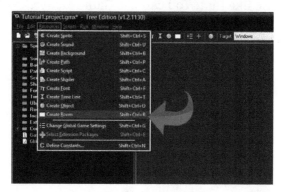

4. Put your game all together now. Create rooms (which can be thought of as levels or menus) and load your objects into them. You can design backgrounds for them, also. Make sure that you test it a few times at every few changes that you make, so that you're not too confused later if something goes wrong.

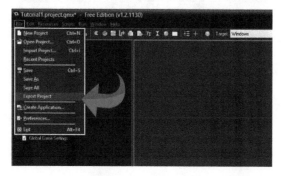

5. Export your game and send it to friends by attaching it to e-mails. You can even keep it on your own computer on the desktop. Begin playing, and have a fun time.

# How to make a Breakout Game with Game Maker

## Steps

GameMaker: Studio

1. Open Game Maker.

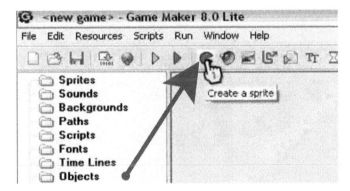

2. Create the following:

- A sprite called spr_paddle.

- A sprite called spr_ball.

- A sprite called spr_wall.

- A sprite called spr_wall_break with a different color than the normal wall.

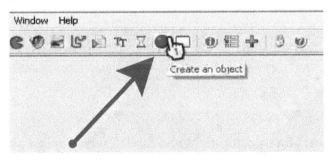

3. Create an object for each with the same names except *obj_* instead of *spr_*. e.g. *obj_paddle* for *spr_paddle*.

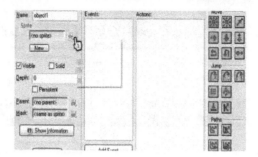

4. For obj_paddle.

- Left key pressed: Move left with a speed of 5.

- Right key pressed: Move right with a speed of 5.

- Any key released: Move nowhere with a speed of 0.

- Collision with wall: move nowhere with a speed of 0.

- Check the *solid* box.

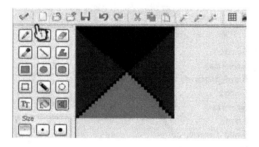

5. For obj_wall.

- Check the *solid* box.

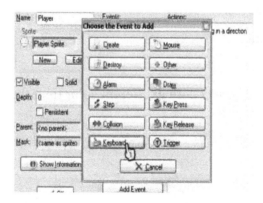

6. For obj_ball.

- In the create event: Move up, top right and top left with a speed of 4.

- In collision with wall: Bounce off solid objects.

- Collision with wall break: Bounce off solid objects. Set the score to 10 and check the *relative* box. Destroy other.

- Collision with bat: Bounce off solid objects.

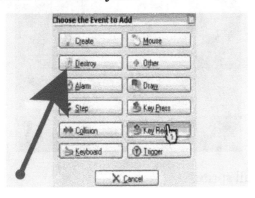

7. For obj_wall_break.

- Collision with ball: Destroy self.

## How to make a Platform Game in Game Maker

**Steps**

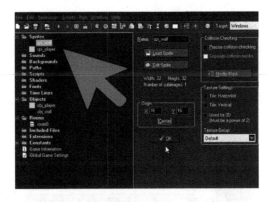

1. Make a simple block sprite for your wall. Also make a sprite for your player. For the wall call it spr_wall and the player spr_player.

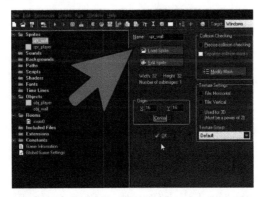

2. Make an object called obj_wall and check the solid box.

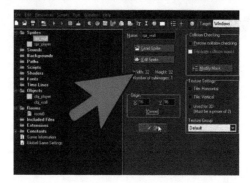

3. Make sure you select the wall sprite.

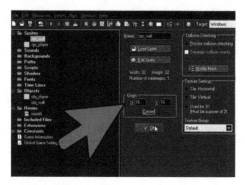

4. Make an object and call it obj_player.

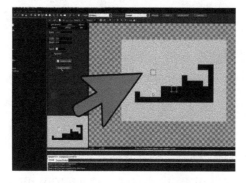

5. Make sure you select your player sprite.

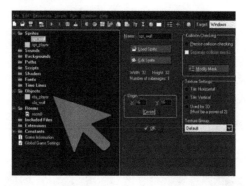

6. For obj_player: go to add event and click Step then Step again. Then go to the control tab, and drag and drop the 'execute code' action.

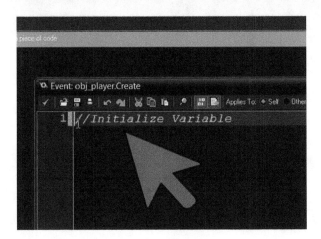

7. Now in the code box put in `// simple Platforming code.// if place_free(x,y+1) { gravity = 0.7 gravity_direction = 270 } else { gravity=0 gravity_direction = 270 } //the arrow keys<,>,^ if place_free(x-4,y)and keyboard_check(vk_left){x-=4} if place_free(x+4,y)and keyboard_check(vk_right){x+=4} if .place_free(x,y+1) and keyboard_check(vk_up){vspeed=-10}`

8. Just copy and paste.

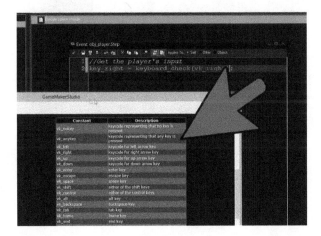

9. For obj_player: Go to add event, then Collision, then with obj_wall.

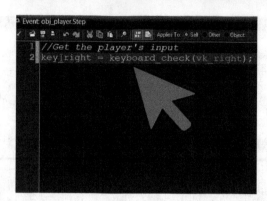

10. Put in this code (go to the control tab and drag and drop 'execute code': move_contact_solid(-direction,12); vspeed=0.

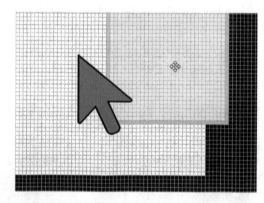

11. Make a room, call it room_1, make a level design by clicking with the selected object and save the room.

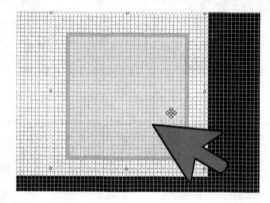

12. Run the game.

# Permissions

# Index

www.ingramcontent.com/pod-product-compliance
Lightning Source LLC
Jackson TN
JSHW052213130125
77033JS00004B/238